Many blessings on your adventure of marriage!
Laura Taggart

making
love last

divorce-proofing your young marriage

LAURA TAGGART,
MA, LMFT

Revell
a division of Baker Publishing Group
Grand Rapids, Michigan

© 2017 by Laura Taggart

Published by Revell
a division of Baker Publishing Group
P.O. Box 6287, Grand Rapids, MI 49516-6287
www.revellbooks.com

Printed in the United States of America

Library of Congress Cataloging-in-Publication Data is on file at the Library of Congress, Washington, DC.

978-0-8007-2785-7

The names and details of the people and situations described in this book have been changed or presented in composite form in order to ensure the privacy of those with whom the author has worked.

Published in association with Books & Such Literary Agency, 52 Mission Circle, Suite 122 PMB 170, Santa Rosa, CA 94509-7953.

17   18   19   20   21   22   23   7   6   5   4   3   2   1

For my husband, Gary.
My partner in life and love.
I'm so glad you said "I do."

Contents

Contents

Foreword

Falling in love is easy! Yet, as many of us well know, staying happily married over a lifetime is another story. As we struggle, resentments build, contempt creeps in, and once sturdy relational bridges are ultimately burned to the ground. If you once were madly in love but now find yourself drifting toward relational disappointment and disillusionment, take heart, because wonderful help begins just a few pages away in Laura Taggart's new book *Making Love Last*.

As we travel and speak around the world, one of our greatest pleasures is getting to meet many amazing people who share a common passion for helping families thrive. On one such trip to the San Francisco Bay Area we had the pleasure of being the guest of Laura Taggart, who was the director of Marriage and Family Ministries at Community Presbyterian Church of Danville. With a passion to help relationships grow and flourish, she founded a marriage mentoring ministry to help young couples navigate the ups and downs of early marriage by being mentored by a more seasoned couple.

Laura has a great heart for families, and as a licensed marriage and family therapist she has the education and experience to offer wise, comprehensive, practical counsel. A teacher at heart, Laura has shared these insights from her therapy office of thirty years, as an adjunct professor at Fuller Theological Seminary, at the Evangelical Theological College in Ethiopia, and now in this new book.

Our working relationship became a personal friendship with Laura and her husband, Gary. As our relationship deepened we discovered Laura and Gary had grown tremendously through the difficulties in their own marriage and honored the covenant they made years ago. We love authors who have success in their own relationships before offering insight to others.

When we first received a copy of *Making Love Last*, we knew we would find wisdom, insight, vulnerability, and practical application. And as we read the manuscript for the first time, Laura surpassed all our expectations. She gives young couples a realistic picture of marriage and the skills to manage difficult seasons. In part 1 she helps couples explore important concepts of married life and challenges them to think about what has influenced their beliefs about marriage. Part 2 will help husbands and wives develop awareness and change the way they relate to one another. Part 3 will help couples create an entirely new vision for their relationship. Discussion questions and suggestions for application make this a practical and life transforming book.

Laura has a special interest in the millennial generation. Many in this age group are marrying in their late twenties, having taken the time to "find themselves" and develop their careers and talents before they commit to marriage. Conventional thought would lead one to believe that married life might be easier when a person marries later in life and has had more time to mature. Yet, as Laura points out, marriage is usually more challenging than we imagined because it *exposes weaknesses* we weren't aware of as singles. She follows up by shedding light on the opportunities for growth and healing that marriage brings and helps couples travel the road of transformation as they help each other heal, change, and grow.

We couldn't be more enthusiastic about Laura Taggart's book *Making Love Last*. So turn the page, begin reading, and discover hope and encouragement that will refresh your mind and soul. Many blessings on your journey of love!

Milan and Kay Yerkovich,
authors of *How We Love* and *How We Love Our Kids*

Acknowledgments

I am deeply indebted to those who personally and professionally supported me through this project and, through their candid feedback, helped to shape this to be a sharper, more helpful book. My dear friend Suzanne Woods Fisher has been my mentor in all things writing and I am so very grateful for her love, candor, wit, and friendship. A very busy and prolific author herself, she has always made time to answer my questions and give me support. She has believed in me, challenged me, guided me, and inspired me. I could not have written this book without her.

I have had the incredible joy of working with several millennials in the shaping of this book. They have generously given of their time and heart to help this book be more engaging, relatable, and helpful. My dear friend and colleague Teagan Darnell has offered her deeply insightful perspective to shape the content and tenor of the book. My amazing niece, Lindsey Norman, gave me great feedback on content and helped edit the early chapters. Nikki Pritchett, a wise and wonderful young mom, carved out time between work and children to read and help me sharpen each chapter. I was so honored that these three incredible women believed in this book and devoted themselves so wholeheartedly to bringing it to life.

I am appreciative of dear friends and fellow therapists who reviewed a chapter and contributed their thoughts: Marilyn Hunt, Ginny Mosby, Brian Kay, and Dave Rohrbach. I am also grateful to all my wonderful friends and fellow therapists at Community Presbyterian Counseling Center for their continual encouragement and support.

I offer my deep gratitude to my friends Milan and Kay Yerkovich, whose profoundly helpful understanding of attachment imprints in couples has impacted my clinical work and writing. Many thanks to Clifford and Joyce Penner for their expertise regarding human sexuality and Joyce's guidance for chapter 9.

I want to thank Toni Herbine-Blank for her mentorship and role in reshaping my thoughts on couples therapy. It was a privilege to be the student of such a warm and gifted teacher. Her insights on applying Internal Family Systems to couples in her Intimacy from the Inside Out model have given substance to chapter 4.

I am indebted to Richard Schwartz for his origination of the Internal Family Systems model of therapy, to Ken Sande for his thoughts on apologies, to Ellyn Bader and Peter Pearson for their developmental model of treating couples, and to Tim Keller for his theological understanding of marriage.

I am profoundly grateful to the couples whom I have had the privilege of counseling over the years. They have taught me about the tenacity of the human spirit and have had the courage to expose their pain and allow me to walk alongside them. I also appreciate those who took the time to take the Making Love Last survey. This survey helped to shape chapters 4–9, offering practical help to young couples.

I am grateful to Kathy Ide and Lindsey Spoolstra for their incisive editing. My dear friend Diane Camp was also instrumental in helping me edit and shape chapter 1 and has been a great encourager.

My husband, Gary, has been a huge support from the time of early conception to the present. Although birthing our two beautiful children together is far more miraculous and creative than any book could ever be, as with our children, I could not have given birth to this book without him. I am grateful for his constant belief in me, his love and encouragement, and his patience with the mess on the dining room table.

I am grateful for my adult children: Emily—for always pushing me to reach beyond my comfort zones and be a better mom and person. Tim—for your generous heart and wisdom beyond your years.

I want to extend my deep gratitude to my parents, Bud and June Naslund, and their courageous journey through their own marriage challenges. They inspired me to become a marriage and family therapist by the way they fought for their marriage and came to enjoy the sweet fruit produced by years of weeding and watering.

Finally, I want to thank those who have believed in me and in this book. Your confidence has been humbling and inspiring. I am so very grateful to my editor, Andrea Doering, for her guidance in shaping the direction of the book, her wisdom, and her willingness to say yes. I feel so fortunate to have Wendy Lawton as my agent. She has been a great encourager and helped me to see the bigger picture of being a writer.

Introduction

This book is the fruit of three experiences of my life: my thirty years of being a marital therapist, my role as director of marriage and family ministry at a large church, and my own marriage of forty years.

When my husband and I were married, we were very young and in love. We were excited to begin creating our shared life and looked forward to enjoying adventures, experiencing milestones, and building our dream together. We expected that there might be some mild adjustments that would need to be made but believed our love was certainly strong enough to overcome any challenges we faced.

We had no idea what lay ahead.

Year seven was particularly painful. The glow of our shiny polished idealizations had faded, and we were deep in the trenches of disappointed expectations and self-protective patterns of relating. My husband wasn't the guy I'd expected him to be, and I wasn't the woman he had married. The reality of married life had hit, and we weren't too happy about it.

But things changed. And as I look back over the seasons of our married life, I realize we have had many marriages within our marriage—our idealized early years, our period of disillusionment and disconnection, our later season of reconnection and mutual support, and our current time of enjoying the fruit of our hard work. It hasn't been easy. And we could never have envisioned that what we enjoy today could even be possible in the earlier, more difficult years.

When you said "I do," you likely didn't have any idea you had just embarked on the greatest crucible of your life. You may have come to marriage with idealized expectations of how life would be with your spouse. Like most of us who marry, you long for a lifelong marriage to your best friend but you may feel unprepared as to how to navigate the failed expectations and ensuing disillusionment.

Today, young marrieds have a 32 percent divorce/separation rate. Many feel ill-equipped to handle the conflict that comes with marriage and may assume that it must indicate they've married "the wrong one."

In my role as the director of marriage and family ministry at Community Presbyterian Church in Danville, California, I have met with dozens of young couples struggling to hold their marriages together. They sought marriage mentors—older, more seasoned couples who had strong, Christian marriages and were trained to come alongside young marrieds to help them set a firm foundation. Many of these young couples had no healthy model of what marriage could look like and had already begun to experience negative patterns and disillusionment. They desired to have a marriage that was all God intended it to be but didn't know the path to get there.

In preparation for writing this book, I conducted a survey of 256 young marrieds (those married less than ten years). Some of their comments reflect these unexpected challenges as they relayed what was most surprising to them:

> "Feeling like you don't even know the person you're married to and knowing that if you were not fully committed, it would be way too easy to leave."
>
> "Marriage has revealed to me how selfish I am and how deeply my actions, or lack thereof, can affect my husband."

"When we first got married I thought I was good at communicating, but no one prepared me for how different it was to communicate with a *wife*."

"How the little stuff can become big stuff so quickly."

"How quickly the 'young love' turns into the 'old couple.' I feel like we have to schedule sex just to make it happen, while we used to be so spontaneous and romantic."

"That the person I chose to marry ended up being someone I would fight and argue with. I've never been one to argue or not get along with anyone, but my husband and I don't see eye to eye on much."

"How our pasts, our upbringings, and our families would have far-reaching influence on our marriage."

"How quickly we can become disconnected because of our busyness and activities."

"I didn't imagine how compromising would be as hard as it can be sometimes."

"How much I miss my alone time, and even when I get 'me' time, I feel guilty and neglectful."

"How hard it would be to balance the exhaustion of raising children with being available to my husband."

"How much the daily grind chips away at romance."

"That we would be dealing with a sex addiction."

"I thought we'd be more 'in love' and 'on cloud nine' for longer than we were. Marriage was more work sooner than I was expecting."

"Dealing with in-laws!"

"That finances would be such a hot topic with heated discussions."

Do any of these sound familiar? If you're reading this book, you may have discovered that marriage is hard work. Perhaps you can relate to the dashed expectations and have lingering thoughts that you and your mate may not be "compatible." You may be wondering how you went from the bliss of the wedding to the degree of disconnection and conflict you are currently experiencing. If so, this book is for you.

For over thirty years, I have counseled countless young couples. It seems that now, more than ever, couples are calling it quits when they face the difficulties of married life. Many have had no real model of what a healthy, thriving marriage looks like, which feeds their level of disillusionment. The problem for these couples is not that they have lost the desire to have a deeply satisfying and loving marriage. The problem is they don't trust that change is possible and they have lost the resiliency necessary to give change a chance.

Change is possible, and this book will help you dive in and enjoy its benefits. Think of the potential change ahead as a flowing river. You can watch it go by and never put a toe in, or you can grab an inner tube and jump in. Along the way you will notice some new scenery, and when you step out onto dry land from time to time, you'll realize you're in a new place. Marriage is dynamic and ever-changing. The potential for growth is part of the DNA of marriage itself.

Each of my experiences—my own marriage, my role in ministry, and my years as a therapist—have given me a deep affection for struggling young couples. They have also led me to a growing passion to help these couples through their difficult seasons.

■ ■ ■

Making Love Last will help young couples divorce-proof their marriage and enjoy a thriving lifelong relationship with their best friend. In part 1, "Reimagining Marriage," I will explore how you think about marriage. Chapter 1 will examine idealized expectations of marriage and address why marriage is such hard work. Rather than seeing problems as evidence of failure, you will see the value of marital difficulties as not only normal but necessary to a strong marriage. Chapter 2 will explore current values that conflict with marital happiness and set a couple up for disillusionment.

It will offer new ways of thinking that will support both your uniqueness as an individual and the growing bond of your marriage. Chapter 3 offers a fresh perspective on the unique benefits of marriage and why your marriage is worthy of your investment. Part 2, "Revitalizing Marriage," will give you six action steps that will enable you to change the way you relate with your spouse. Chapter 4 will start with a deep and honest look at yourself. You will be given tools to explore your ways of being in relationship and ways of understanding the impact of your upbringing. Chapter 5 will help you to explore the differences between you and your mate. Rather than feeling threatened by the way in which your mate is different from you, you will become aware of the vitality those differences bring to your marriage and be encouraged to embrace them.

In the early stage of married life, you may have tried to suppress conflict. It does not fit the picture of what happy couples do. Many young couples tend to avoid bringing up touchy or difficult subjects, and many feel unskilled at working through conflict successfully. Chapter 6 will provide tools to proactively enter into conflict in a way that decreases hurt and increases understanding. Out of hurt, habit, or a need to feel secure, couples often hold on to habits that damage their relationship and keep them stuck. Chapter 7 will address the habits you may be clinging to and give you a way to release them and enjoy life with your best friend.

It is not big vacations or extravagant gifts that cement the connection of thriving marriages. It is the small increments of behavior that make the difference. Every moment you share with your spouse, you either lean in to the relationship or lean out. When you lean in, you nourish positive connection. Becoming aware of these opportunities to lean in is the focus of chapter 8.

Marriage is intended to provide the deepest human companionship of your life. This intimacy involves being vulnerable with your emotional, sexual, and spiritual selves. Chapter 9 will address some of the hindrances to closeness you may be experiencing and offer specific help to ignite your intimate connection.

When we say "I do," we promise to love for a lifetime. Although we have no idea about what that "labor of love" will entail, we commit ourselves to the road ahead. Chapter 10 will explore the beauty of a covenant marriage and challenge the contingencies we often allow to influence our marriage commitment.

When we focus on our mate's deficiencies, our relationships suffer. When we begin to see the difficult, even painful parts of our marriages as an impetus for our own growth, change and healing begin to happen. Chapter 11 explores how God uses marriage as a catalyst for change in our own lives and how his love can release us to experience more freedom in our relationships.

Young couples need a vision of what it looks like to be married to our best friend for a lifetime. As a parent, I have often heard the anonymous quote, "There are only two lasting bequests we can hope to give our children. One of these is roots; the other, wings." A thriving marriage is also about roots and wings. To keep the tree steady in tumultuous storms, we need a strong set of roots that sink deep into the soil to hold us firm. We also want to help each other become all we were meant to be, to help each other fly.

If chapters 10 and 11 are about the roots that keep you steady in the storms, chapter 12 will help you to take flight as a couple in such a way that you are inspired to become your best selves—and in the process, best friends. It will help you cast a vision for your future together that will help you move forward into the lasting, loving marriage you desire.

It is my sincere hope that in these pages you will be encouraged, understood, challenged, and inspired to experience the extraordinary richness of married life. If you are hoping to deepen the bond you have with your mate, this book is for you. You will find new perspectives and skills that will help you create the intimate marriage you long for. If you are discouraged and despairing, wondering if your marriage can recover, hold on and read. The road ahead will not be easy but it may surprise you.

PART 1

Reimagining Marriage—Changing the Way You Think

1

Why Marriage
Is Hard Work

What counts in making a happy marriage is not so much how
compatible you are, but how you deal with incompatibility.

Leo Tolstoy

It was late in the afternoon on a hot, muggy August day. James
and Amy were my last appointment. They were new clients, a
young married couple who were considering divorce. They sat on
opposite sides of the couch in my office, barely looking at each
other. Everything about James oozed hostility—legs extended,
arms crossed against his chest. Amy curled into the couch corner
as if to protect tender wounds.

I started the session by asking how they met, hoping to awaken
their sense of earlier connection. Amy brightened and took the
lead. "Oh, that's a good story," she said. "We both loved soccer
and were playing for a co-ed league. We were on different teams
but I noticed him. Later in the game I blocked his shot on goal
and he gave me heck for it."

"It was a great shot," James said, leaning forward. "She was in the right place at the right time."

This was the first stirring of interest I had noticed in James. "Tell me about your wedding," I said, encouraged by the slight drop in tension.

"It was a beautiful day," Amy said. "Everything went perfectly."

"Except for your drunken uncle," James said.

Amy shot a scowl at him. "The wedding *was* perfect."

I jumped in. "So when did things start to go wrong?" I looked at James.

"I'd say a couple of years ago," James said. "My work started to become more demanding. At first, Amy was pretty understanding, but after a while she became really critical about it."

"It wasn't just his work," Amy said. "He was going out with the guys almost every weekend. I was alone a lot. When I'd complain, he'd tell me I was trying to control him." She slumped back in her corner. "Over time, I just felt misunderstood and hopeless."

As the story unfolded, it became clear that the initial dream they'd shared for their life together was shattering. Early in the relationship they had enjoyed shared interests, a strong romantic connection, and similar ambitions. Amy had been willing to subordinate her desire for time with James. Eventually, she had become very disappointed with his lack of attentiveness and his priorities of work and friends. In her hurt, she became critical and pulled away emotionally and physically.

James felt deprived; their sexual intimacy had taken a nosedive and he felt he could never do anything right. He, in turn, pulled away and spent longer hours at work to avoid the tension at home. They had dreamed of being married to their best friend for life. Four years later, they were considering divorce.

After James and Amy's appointment, I felt sad. Over the previous five years, I had noticed a significant rise in the number of troubled young marrieds who came into my office seeking help. A nationwide study on first marriages of 22,682 individuals ages

15–44 in the United States confirmed my concern. As reported in the *National Health Statistics Reports* in March 2012, 20 percent of marriages end in the first five years and 32 percent end in the first 10 years.[1] Couples married five to ten years represent the greatest increase in divorce rate in any five-year period.

Perhaps this has caused you concern. You may be feeling pretty good about your marriage currently, but as you hear these statistics and look around and see other couples who appear to be happy as well, you wonder if you could end up being one of the 32 percent. Things are good now, but you want to make sure your relationship stays healthy, strong, and resilient. You want to be preemptive and keep your relationship on track. Or perhaps you have begun to have significant struggles.

The problems and complaints I hear vary to some degree but have a common thread: the couples feel ill-equipped to handle the realities of married life. When problems hit and expectations are dashed, they have no capacity to navigate issues in a way that is not damaging to the relationship. It is as if they have been given a car but have only a limited amount of gas and no equipment to fix a flat tire. At a time when they could be enjoying the trip together and planning for their future, the car has stalled out.

Perhaps you can relate. In your early dating days, you enjoyed getting to know each other and discovering mutual interests. Over time you fell in love and couldn't picture your life without your future mate. When you married, you hoped to share a long life with your best friend. You deeply longed for meaningful relationship, intimacy, and companionship. You may have had a glimpse of some differences between you and your mate but overlooked them as you were moving toward the future.

And then, at some point, things began to take a turn. Qualities you used to find endearing in your spouse became annoying. The differences you used to overlook started to threaten the togetherness you hoped to enjoy. In an effort to change the course of dissatisfaction, one or both of you challenged the behavior or habits of the other, stirring a negative reaction. This began a cycle of repeating the negative interaction over and over until a sense of hopelessness settled like a dark cloud over your marriage.

As I counsel young couples, the questions they ask are similar to those asked by James and Amy:

> "If we love each other, why do we struggle so much?"
>
> "Why didn't someone tell us marriage would be this hard?"
>
> "What if I didn't have a good role model for how to work through problems?"
>
> "How can we do conflict in a healthier way?"

These questions reveal a desire to discover a path *through* the difficulties so they can enjoy the gift that marriage is meant to be.

Marriage is hard work for many reasons. You may have come to marriage with idealized expectations of how life would be with your mate, only to become disillusioned when problems surfaced. Not knowing how to cope with the disillusionment, you may find yourself confused, angry, and wondering how to move forward.

Another reason marriage is hard work is that, most likely, you come from very different backgrounds. Even if you share similar values or come from the same geographic area, your families of origin are dissimilar, and you each bring different interpretations and meanings to marriage from your experiences. These differing vantage points are often surprising to discover, as people naturally tend to overlook or minimize differences when they're dating.

By nature, we tend to be self-protective in the way we relate to others, and navigating conflict and tension can be difficult, especially when the conflict style of our mate is different from our own. It is important to explore each of these challenges to understand why marriage is such hard work.

But first, it is helpful to know you are not alone. Marriage is hard work for most couples.

Idealizations and Their Impact

As a young couple, you come to marriage with a picture of how it will be. This picture is a composite of beliefs about what a happy marriage looks like—such as the belief that you should have little conflict and much agreement, and that your mate will have few flaws and sustain undivided devotion to you. Often this picture is embellished by media that manufacture fantastic notions of intense and passionate romance.

It can be helpful to know that nearly everyone is surprised by the realities of married life. Your early picture does not usually include navigating competing needs, coping with daily stresses, or dealing with heated conflict. You may have thought that the same ease of conversation and desire to please—so obvious in most dating relationships—will smooth over any difference of opinion or behavior you may experience in the future. In short, you come to marriage with a dream of how your marriage will be.

The dream may be something that has been developing since childhood or of more recent making, but usually it begins to surface as you seek out a partner. The quest for a mate, a life partner with whom to build a future, is universal. Choosing the *right* partner becomes of paramount importance.

Most of us had a picture of what we were looking for in a mate. What was your picture? What were the most important qualities you were seeking in your future spouse? Perhaps you were looking for someone who was ambitious enough to provide a stable financial future. Maybe you wanted a person who would share your love for adventure, your value of family, or your spirituality. You may have sought a person who was thoughtful and kind or gregarious and social. But the truth is, no matter how well suited you might seem, you and your mate are not completely compatible.

There is no such thing as two truly compatible people. That might be a jarring statement for you. Yes, two people can enjoy shared interests and preferences, but all of us have our own histories, experiences, biases, gender-based differences, and physiologies. All individuals are uniquely different. When we seek out a life partner, we may seek someone who is not very different from us but, in truth, they *will* be very different from us. There will be incompatibilities. These incompatibilities will require adjustment and change.

In a study done by the National Marriage Project, young adults were asked what they meant by the word *compatible*. The number one factor for men was someone who was willing "to take them as they are and not try to change them."[2] This would suggest that a compatible marriage should require no change, no accommodation to the other, and no growth, since you are so perfectly suited. Although the desire to feel accepted and adequate is, at one level, understandable, the reality is that any intimate relationship is going to compel change in both parties.

There is no such thing as two truly compatible people.

When you vow to take your mate "for better or for worse" you are accepting not only your mate's flaws but also the changes and adaptations that lie ahead. Change is inevitable in any truly intimate relationship.

A concept that is widespread in our culture is that of the "soul mate." When considering a life partner, you tend to look for that one person in the world that is uniquely designed for you, one who can perfectly mirror your thoughts, feelings, and needs. You assume that there is someone out there who is just right for you and if you look hard enough and long enough you are bound to find them. Once you find them, they will be a perfect "fit" for your life—someone who will meet your needs, support your goals, and be "low maintenance." This pursuit of a soul mate has deluded many into endless searches and marital dissatisfaction.

Consider Amy and James, my clients. Amy believed she had married her soul mate. She had assumed that a truly loving relationship meant that James would be attuned to her need for time with him. When work became more demanding for James, she hoped he would notice her patience and make a special effort to initiate a date night. When he failed to acknowledge her sacrifice or plan time together, she would express her dissatisfaction with a critical jab or moody withdrawal. Her soul mate was not reading her thoughts, which she interpreted as a sign of waning love. Her search for the perfectly compatible mate led to disillusionment when she discovered that she had married a flawed human being who *would* disappoint her.

Idealized expectations can begin as early as the wedding planning itself and can also set a couple up for disillusionment. Now more than ever, the $55 billion wedding industry preys on a bride's happily-ever-after fantasies, and the more money spent, the better. A study by popular wedding planning website The Knot found that the average US wedding cost in 2014 was $31,213.[3] Brides are being sold on the idea that they must stage an extravagant wedding that reflects their personal sense of style, such as commissioning artists to paint a custom backdrop for the ceremony or hiring social media consultants to make sure photos are posted and tagged accurately. The meaning of the day can get lost in the preoccupation of planning the day.

The wedding is an important day, but it is only one day. As brides (and grooms, though to a lesser degree) find themselves caught up in the creation of their perfect day, they focus less on preparing for the relational, emotional, and spiritual aspects of their marriage. Premarital counseling may have helped you anticipate some of these crucial aspects; after all, every wedding is followed by a marriage. The idealization around the wedding often causes couples to overlook important relational issues, which will inevitably surface as real life returns. Although your wedding day has likely passed, the planning season could have initiated some early patterns of expectation and disillusionment that may need addressing.

Idealistic expectations involve more than unrealistic thinking about finding the perfect mate and planning the perfect day. The "soul mate" concept also suggests that once you find this person you will be so connected, so able to mirror each other, that there will be little to no conflict. Most people, when they marry, have an understanding that they will have some disagreements but cannot imagine having relationship-threatening levels of conflict. They trust that, because they are so well suited, they will bypass the really serious conflicts experienced by their parents or others they've known. And if they do have problems, they will be resolved quickly.

After all, in an age where technology sends the message that the solution is at your fingertips, the belief is that things should get better fast, including problems in marriage. Getting an instantaneous fix is much preferred to waiting and doing the hard work of resolution. When difficulties don't remedy quickly, young couples often assume their marriage is in trouble. The idealization that a happy marriage is a conflict-free zone causes them to believe their marriage is failing when arguing persists.

When James and Amy entered my office, their idealizations about marriage had taken their toll. Their picture of finding a soul mate had begun to unravel. Their levels of conflict had surpassed their expectations and capacities to cope. They felt unprepared for the difficulties of working out real life with a real person. The misconception that marriage is easier than it is led them to early disillusionment and thoughts of exiting their marriage. Contributing to their difficulties was the common challenge of navigating the differences inherent in two different upbringings.

The Blending of Two Family Histories

When you marry, you are focused on the shared life you intend to build together. Similarities and the joining of two dreams into one occupy your thoughts. There is a tendency to suppress differences for the sake of keeping the dream alive. Over time, tensions begin to mount as misunderstandings occur. This is inevitable for two people whose perspectives have been shaped by different families of origin.

My client James said he came from a family that tolerated clutter. As long as his dad could find the remote control for the television, very little attention was paid to order in the home. There were minimal expectations that the children would do chores or even pick up after themselves. By necessity James learned to wash his own clothes by the time he was ten. He never knew which parent would drive him to school or when he would be picked up.

In contrast, Amy's mom was very particular about the cleanliness of the home. Amy and her sister were given clear guidelines about what was expected when they performed their chores of cleaning bathrooms, washing dishes, doing laundry, and scrubbing floors. She expected the girls to keep their bedrooms clean at all times. A list of consequences for the occasional undone chore or messy bedroom was posted on the refrigerator door.

When James and Amy married, they rented an apartment and enjoyed fixing it up with new finds from IKEA. James worked as a programmer in high tech, and Amy taught at the local elementary school. Amy typically got home earlier than James and enjoyed cleaning and organizing the home. Initially James had enjoyed Amy's organization and her efforts in keeping the apartment picked up, but eventually, when the demands of work meant he felt exhausted when he arrived home, he wanted to enjoy a more relaxed atmosphere, which included throwing his personal items wherever they landed. Amy grew irritated with his carelessness. When her attempts at correcting his behavior were not received well, she resorted to labeling him as selfish and slovenly. Their two family histories set them up for a collision of needs that became a source of ongoing daily tension.

Every couple has adjustments to make in marriage due to differences in family backgrounds. These differences include the way things are done, the priority given to certain protocols, and varying interpretations and meanings assigned to specific words and behaviors.

Sean and Michelle, another young couple who were clients of mine, were struggling to work through their unique upbringings. Sean had grown up in a very competitive family with two athletic brothers. When his dad would take them to the tennis court, they would do drills before game time and compete to beat the next older sibling.

Michelle had grown up as an only child with little experience of team play and lots of affirmation for her piano-playing skills. She enjoyed an occasional game of tennis but played mostly for the social connection and for fun.

When Sean would suggest to Michelle, "Let's play tennis," it meant something very different to each of them. He hoped for an aggressively played match and ultimate victory while she sought connection. She felt intimidated by Sean's competitive spirit. This difference in meaning led them to not only abandon tennis but all other sports and games that might have enhanced their mutual enjoyment. In short, every couple has challenges to negotiate in order to maximize mutual enjoyment of one another and of life. This does, however, make marriage a challenging adjustment.

Self-Protection and the Impact of Childhood Wounds

Perhaps the most difficult hurdle for young marrieds to overcome, the one that creates the most hardship, is the self-protective ways they relate to one another. These are so difficult because they are not easily recognized in yourself but are very apparent in your spouse. Whereas idealizations create disillusionment and differences in family backgrounds create misunderstanding and frustration, self-protective ways of relating create hurt and distance from your partner.

Remember James? He grew up in a family where emotions were viewed as weak. He remembers crying when he was five because his brother stole his tricycle. His father responded by telling him, "You keep that up, and I'll give you something to cry about." His mother, likewise, was not emotive; she didn't invite James to express his feelings or wants. He learned early on to suppress his emotions, and over time he even learned to disregard them altogether. He applied himself in school, which garnered him some limited affirmation from his parents. Although he was more athletic than his brother, his talent drew little notice from his parents. They chose not to attend any of his high school soccer games. They were busy "making a living," or so he was told.

Whereas idealizations create disillusionment and differences in family backgrounds create misunderstanding and frustration, self-protective ways of relating create hurt and distance from your partner.

Amy grew up with a mom whose expectations were difficult to meet. Her dad was very consumed with his work and often unavailable. Although Amy was a good student, she remembered the look of disappointment on her mother's face if she failed to bring home all A's. Amy's mother was very present in her childhood, she recalled, but also very stressed, not the kind of parent a child could easily confide in. Amy found herself longing for her dad to show more interest in spending time with her and remembers with vivid clarity the few special times they shared.

Both James and Amy had wounds from childhood that were hidden from their conscious awareness. Amy's desire to have meaningful conversations, to spend regular time with James where she had his undivided attention, was initially well received by him. He enjoyed being desired and also enjoyed Amy's warm responsiveness when he focused on her.

But it wasn't long before James started to feel smothered by Amy's desire for togetherness and began to view her as "needy." He was unaware of his own disconnection from his feelings and protected himself by disregarding Amy's feelings. Having grown up in an emotionally disengaged family, he experienced a great deal of discomfort with Amy's longing for intimate connection. His self-protective style of relating, well-honed from his youth, led him to push her away and seek out less "demanding" relationships with male friends. Feeling ill-equipped to meet Amy's needs, he invested himself in the one environment where he felt most capable, his work.

Amy was also unaware of the wound that was impacting her responses to her husband. During courtship and early marriage, Amy believed she had found that special someone who would give her the attention and affirmation she longed for. James enjoyed surprising her with special adventures—a picnic dinner in the park overlooking the bay, front-row seats to the professional soccer game. With the juggle of two jobs and limited funds, these outings became infrequent. At first, Amy would hint to remind James to plan time together. In the past year, those nudges had escalated to reactive outbursts. Amy's responses, triggered by her father's sporadic attention and her mother's disapproval, revealed her deep wounds.

Neither James nor Amy were aware that their responses toward their mate had their roots in their childhood experiences. Both blamed the other. James blamed Amy's "neediness" for his avoidance; Amy blamed James's negligence for her reactivity. They both felt completely justified in their entrenched positions—but they were stuck. Without an awareness of the underlying pain fueling their responses, they were unable to develop compassion for themselves or for each other—an awareness they would need to extricate themselves from their impasse.

The Strength That Comes by Fire

Marriage is likely to be the most challenging thing any two people will ever undertake. It is also the most rewarding. Because it is the most intimate relationship of your life, it has the power to evoke the deepest emotions and expose tender vulnerabilities.

If you have the courage to examine the imprint of your upbringing and the way it impacts your responses to your mate, you will be choosing a path that not only deepens your self-awareness but also brings compassion and understanding to your marriage. If you are able to approach the differences in your family backgrounds as normal, even interesting, you will be able to use them to enhance your relationship instead of hinder it. If you can identify the idealizations you have that are creating dissatisfaction and release them so you can embrace the real mate you married—with all their imperfections—your marital happiness will increase.

Much like fire is needed to burn off the impurities of a precious nugget of gold, a beautiful marriage requires the heat of challenges to mature into a more compassionate, loving, and fulfilling relationship. As the dross of idealized expectations, impugning of differences, and self-protective styles of relating are exposed to the heat, what emerges is something quite unexpected—a shiny, solid treasure in which you can see yourself, your mate, and your marriage itself in a new way.

> *Much like fire is needed to burn off the impurities of a precious nugget of gold, a beautiful marriage requires the heat of challenges to mature into a more compassionate, loving, and fulfilling relationship.*

Yes, marriage is hard. Taking two individuals with their own habits, histories, beliefs, preferences, experiences, and wounds and adding the pressures and stresses of life is difficult at best. To believe differently is to set yourself up for failure. The good news—no, the *great* news—is there's a much bigger picture. Marriage has higher purposes than you can even imagine! And your imagination—the way you think about and picture marriage—is vitally important to how you navigate the road ahead. In the next chapter, I'll explore some new ways of thinking about marriage that will help you move toward that awesome, epic marriage you and your spouse long for.

Discussion Questions: Chapter 1

Group and Couple Questions

1. How can being "compatible" benefit a marriage? How can concepts of compatibility be detrimental to a marriage?

2. Have you ever thought that you have one "soul mate" out of the seven-billion-plus people on the planet? What is tempting about this concept? What is dangerous about "soul mate" thinking?

3. Share three ways in which your different family histories create challenges for you and your spouse.

4. Did you have idealized expectations when you first got married? What were they? What was your first disillusionment? Did you have the idea that marriage would be easy? How do Luke 9:23 and John 16:33 challenge that notion?

5. Why do you think marriage requires hard work? What do 2 Corinthians 4:17, Romans 5:3, and James 1:2–4 say about the purpose of our struggles?

For Personal Reflection

1. When you got married, what was your picture of what a happy marriage looked like?

2. Can you identify any expectations you've had that cause difficulty in your marriage? Have you had any notions about

compatibility or wanting a "soul mate" that have caused disappointment or dissatisfaction in your relationship?

3. Are you aware of any ways in which your family history has contributed to your ways of thinking or behaving that have been a challenge in your marriage relationship?

2

More Than
You Imagined

If you want something new, you have to stop doing something old.

Peter F. Drucker

Imagination is limitless. The creativity of young entrepreneurs and their ingenious ideas are awe-inspiring. Consider these recent inventions: a wearable air purifier, global apps providing instantaneous multilingual translation, and paint that turns smooth surfaces into dry-erase boards. Today's generation is popping up with all kinds of outside-the-box concepts to improve people's lives and connect the planet.

In the wave of these innovative changes, the concept of following the rules has become outdated. One young millennial told me, "The most successful people are the ones who explore and question everything. We've become a generation of outliers." What has gone before is far less compelling than finding and creating your own way. What if all this innovation were applied to relationships? Especially the most important relationship of your life: marriage.

You may have witnessed a lifeless marriage, one in which two individuals simply tolerate each other because it seems easier economically. Or perhaps you've observed a marriage in which a couple feels constrained by beliefs about marriage but lacks the courage to invest in growth and change. You have also likely witnessed a marriage influenced by cultural trends suggesting that if marriage isn't working for you, get out and find someone new while you're still young and "marketable."

Rather than just resigning yourself to an unsatisfying relationship or bailing out if it becomes challenging, what if there was a different way to do marriage?

Whether or not we are able to enjoy the richness of married life and navigate its inherent hardships depends on how we think about marriage. *Is my spouse supposed to make me happy? Will I have to give up my independence to make this work? If we have differences, does that mean we are incompatible? Do I think of marriage as a revocable contract? What are my options if I'm unhappy?*

> *Rather than just resigning yourself to an unsatisfying relationship or bailing out if it becomes challenging, what if there was a different way to do marriage?*

Remember James and Amy? They entered their marriage feeling secure that their commitment would withstand the test of time. But when they came in for therapy, that belief had been shaken.

James and Amy realized that trends in their peer culture could be threatening their relationship. The values of success, lifestyle comfort, and personal achievement had tempted James into losing his priority of time with Amy. Amy wanted to be happy, and she assumed that getting her needs met would accomplish that goal.

Having married in their late twenties, James and Amy had enjoyed a great deal of independence prior to marriage. Once married, they found making sacrifices and considering each other's needs difficult. They bristled at the thought of giving up their independent paths to create a union of two lives.

Guarding independence, pursuing novelty, and seeking self-fulfillment are hallmarks of our current culture. Each pose a unique challenge to married couples, since an intimate relationship will require giving these up to some degree.

Guarding independence, pursuing novelty, and seeking self-fulfillment are hallmarks of our current culture. Each pose a unique challenge to married couples, since an intimate relationship will require giving these up to some degree.

Yours, Mine, and Ours

One impact of valuing independence and self-fulfillment is postponing marriage. Most young couples want to get married but choose to wait until they have careers and lifestyles settled. They don't want to select a life partner until they have explored their options. In the survey I conducted of 256 young married millennials, 31 percent indicated that they had lived together before marrying, and of those who did, 36 percent indicated they had done so in order to test their relationship for compatibility—the highest percentage for any reason given.[1] (For more survey results, see appendix E.) Giving up independence is risky. In delaying marriage and testing the waters, some hope to minimize that risk.

This delay impacts a couple's thinking, particularly in the early stages of marriage. In previous generations, couples married young and figured out life together. Much like a start-up business, marriage was where all decisions about careers, family, and finances were made. With more couples wedding in their

43

late twenties and early thirties, marriage has become more like a merger than a start-up.[2]

Stacey and Matt met at a sports bar in San Francisco. Both fans of the Giants, they had each come to the bar with a few friends. Matt was immediately taken with Stacey's energy and quick wit, and she enjoyed his attention. They exchanged phone numbers and went out for dinner the following week.

Matt was impressed with Stacey's rapid rise to become vice president of a strategic planning corporation. She was well organized, articulate, and gifted at envisioning processes necessary to accomplish the company's goals. Matt had recently become a partner in a real estate law firm. Stacey appreciated his dry sense of humor and his knowledge of world events.

They dated sporadically. Stacey traveled for work, and Matt was still involved with another young woman. As their relationship grew more serious, Stacey assumed Matt's affections for her were undivided. Matt knew he needed to say goodbye to his other girlfriend, but he didn't want to hurt her. He also wanted to know Stacey was a "sure thing" before he called it quits. However, Matt's ambivalence caused a major blowup with Stacey. He didn't want to lose her, so he relinquished the other relationship when she found out about it.

After six months of seeing each other exclusively, Matt and Stacey decided to move in together. Both of them had built their own lives, furnished their own apartments, and pursued their own interests. They found it challenging to combine their separate lives.

Fights soon began over whose apartment they would move into and which set of furniture would remain. The familiar turf of each was a reminder of their quest to build a fulfilling life individually, and neither wanted to relinquish their trophies.

Matt and Stacey valued personal independence. They had each developed a social network and expected the other to meld into their group. In deciding which friends would be included in their social calendar, Matt and Stacey frequently went separate ways to sustain already cultivated relationships.

Matt had fulfilled his dream of a rewarding career and hoped to supplement it with an attractive and accomplished wife. Stacey had worked hard to build her life. She sought fulfillment in the relationship but found it difficult to make compromises. Both perceived sacrificing their own needs as diminishing their freedom. A year after moving in together, Matt and Stacey decided to marry. They wanted a child and felt it was "time." They had an extravagant wedding at a winery in Napa. Their difficulty merging their lives was evident during their wedding planning, which I will discuss later.

In a young start-up marriage, you each bring what you have and throw it into the pot to create a future dream together. No prenuptial agreements here. You're both all-in. The future is uncertain but you build your life together from scratch.

Those who marry in their late twenties or thirties may experience the more difficult challenges of a merger marriage. You're both concerned with identifying and protecting what you bring to the relationship. Merging is filled with decisions about the best ways to create a streamlined union. To further complicate matters, you and your mate may have silent expectations, each of you assuming the other partner will adapt to you and your needs.

If you are in a merger marriage, consider creating new beginnings together. In Matt and Stacey's case, they could have decided to find a new apartment and furnish it with a few items each couldn't live without. They could include each other in their decisions and explore developing new traditions as a couple.

Reshaping your thinking to embrace a shared life will stretch you. It will also give you opportunities to create something new and innovative.

Freedom versus Constraint

For most young people, having alternatives is essential and highly valued. Perhaps technology has influenced today's thinking about marriage. With instant access to information and consumer products and apps of every variety, the options seem endless. The idea of being bound to a decision or having choices restricted, particularly by some cultural or religious norm, is dismissed. The risk of making a poor decision is mitigated by the possibility of making a different choice in the future. But keeping options open, though it appeases one's aversion to risk, can carry with it a high degree of anxiety and unhappiness.

Some young people will leave a marriage if it fails to meet their needs or expectations. For them, loyalty is based on satisfaction. *As long as my needs are getting met, I'm in. If not, I'm out!*

External constraints (vows of commitment, the welfare of the children, honoring the institution itself) hold many traditional marriages together. But those things have less power to sustain a struggling young couple when exiting seems easy.

In a TED Talk on "The Surprising Science of Happiness," Harvard psychologist Dan Gilbert stated that we are very focused today on guarding our freedom and throwing off anything that might restrict it.[3] He defined freedom as "the ability to make up your mind and change your mind." We don't like having any constraints put on us that might limit our ability to choose. If we make a mistake, we want the chance to cut our losses and take a new course.

To illustrate his point, Dan shared a study he had conducted at Harvard University that measured happiness as it relates to freedom. He taught a photography class where students were asked to take pictures of meaningful aspects of their lives at Harvard using old-fashioned film cameras. They brought in the negatives and were shown how to use a darkroom. Dan instructed them to enlarge two of their favorite photos and bring them to class the next day. When the students brought them in, he told them to give one up. They had to make a choice between their two favorite pictures.

The students were divided into two groups. One group was told that the decision was irreversible; once they gave up the picture, they could not change their minds. The other group was told they had four days to change their minds. Then some students in each group were asked to make a prediction. How much would they come to like the picture they kept compared to the picture they gave up? Both groups of students expected to like the pictures they kept slightly better.

But what they actually found was that the students who could not change their minds came to like the picture they kept much better. In contrast, the students given the choice to change their minds did *not* like the pictures they kept. Days after the deadline, they remained unhappy with the pictures they kept, regardless of whether they exchanged them during the four-day grace period.

The conclusion from the study was that although most students would prefer to have the freedom to change their minds, that freedom to keep their options open left them ambivalent and dissatisfied. Once their decisions were made and other options were off the table, the students grew to accept and appreciate their choices and were much happier. Although having revocable choices sounded good, making a deliberate and irreversible decision led to higher degrees of satisfaction.

These findings have some interesting applications to marriage. If we view it as a reversible decision, a revocable contract, we are likely to see the imperfections of our mate in an exaggerated light and overidealize other options. As we become dissatisfied with our current choice, the alternatives become unrealistically appealing. On the other hand, if we view marriage as an irreversible decision, accept our choice, and work out the implications of that choice, ultimately we can experience deeper levels of satisfaction.

Is it possible that the "freedom" to keep our options open leads to ambivalence, self-doubt, anxiety, and ultimately unhappiness? Maybe commitment, specifically commitment in marriage, isn't such a bad thing after all.

Self-Fulfillment versus the Fulfillment of a Shared Life

We all desire to feel full of joy, satisfaction, and love. We long to matter, to make a difference in the world, to have an impact on those around us. Leading a well-lived, fulfilling life is important.

Self-fulfillment means different things to different people. To some it means accomplishing a particular goal, making a significant contribution, or successfully reaching their full potential. To others it means gaining a certain status, living a luxurious lifestyle, or satisfying a deep desire.

In the classic Christmas movie *It's a Wonderful Life*, the main character, George, has an idea of what will bring him fulfillment. Tired of living in a small town, he makes plans to see the world. When he falls in love with a local girl, he is frustrated by the likelihood he will have to abandon his dream and settle down. But love prevails, and they marry. On their way to their honeymoon, George's father dies. George inherits the responsibility of running the banking business his father owned, which seems to be yet another blow to his dream. When his uncle loses a significant amount of the company's funds, George falls into despair. As he's ready to jump off a bridge to end his life, an angel intercepts him and shows him the significance of the life he has lived.

The beauty of the movie is in what George realizes at the end. As he dreamed about world travels and material possessions, he'd missed the far deeper fulfillment of loving relationships. While he was contemplating his life as a failure, his faithful friends were collecting funds to defray his financial loss. In the end, George realizes the great treasure of his shared life.

As George discovered, a focus on fulfilling ourselves can deprive us of the love we ultimately long for. Author Tim Keller describes a marriage based on self-fulfillment versus self-denial as one that "will require a low- or no-maintenance partner who meets your needs while making almost no claims on you."[4] The priority of the relationship is on what it can do for you. Does that sound like a recipe for a truly loving marriage?

To enjoy intimate partnership you will need to make room for the needs and desires of your mate. At times they will conflict with yours. To make a marriage work, you will need to learn to give—to bend, postpone, compromise, yield. Your mate will need to do the same.

Many young people believe they should not have to compromise their dreams when they get married. Matt and Stacey had strong ideas as to what their personal strategies for fulfillment were, and although an intimate relationship was important to them, they did not want to subordinate the dreams in which they had invested.

When I helped them probe further, it became clear that each of their identities had been wrapped up in what they had accomplished. Matt had grown up in a home with a highly critical father who never hesitated to point out that Matt couldn't do anything right. Stacey grew up in a home where girls weren't expected to amount to much. For both, their careers were a proving ground and a daily reminder that they had value.

Our initial focus in therapy was to help them articulate their feelings in a way that was not attacking or demeaning. Over the course of a few months, they learned how to have a much different conversation. They were able to slow their interactions and identify the feelings underlying their competing positions. Together, we eventually surfaced the hurt that fueled their insistence on their own fulfillment, and each was able to find compassion for the other's longing to never again feel insignificant or unloved. They began to experience the joy of fulfillment found in relationship.

Rather than competing with each other for priority, you can, in love, support the gifts and dreams of your spouse. Matt was eventually able to invite Stacey to share her heart about what was truly important to her in her career and sought ways to offer her tangible support. As Stacey was able to experience Matt's support of her, she no longer felt compelled to prove herself and was able to show more interest in Matt's hopes and dreams. As they softened, each of them felt more connected and fulfilled. The shared life they hoped for was beginning to become true.

The Pursuit of Happiness

Before you got married, did you expect that marriage would make you happy? Most people believe their wedded lives will be better than when they were single because their mates will provide the emotional and physical companionship they long for—that a spouse will somehow complete them. In short, they are hoping their mates will make them happy.

There are two problems with this perspective. (1) The person you marry is imperfect and is bound to disappoint you. (2) The focus is on *you*. Marriage is much bigger than you. It includes your mate's well-being and has its own creative dynamic that can transform both of you into better people and better lovers.

Our picture of happiness is often too small and shortsighted. Studies have consistently revealed that happiness is not something to be found like the cheese at the end of a maze. It is also not an elusive treasure, forever moving just inches out of reach. Nor is it about having freedom to choose your future. It is not even about the circumstances of your life.

University of California–Berkeley offers an online course called "The Science of Happiness." More than fifty thousand people have taken the course since January 1, 2015, most of whom are millennials (those ages eighteen to thirty-three). They are intensely attracted to the pursuit of happiness and how to achieve it.

One of the instructors, neuroscientist Emiliana Simon-Thomas, stated, "People are hungry for the science of happiness because they've hit a wall in that they've obtained all the things they thought would make them happy, and found themselves still disenchanted."[5] Can you relate? Some people believe that happiness is an absence of hardship, pain, or conflict. Others associate happiness with material success. Many think happiness is linked to keeping their options open and the freedom to choose.

But happiness is not about any of those things. As the course concludes, it is about human connection, acceptance of your life and circumstances, generosity, thankfulness, and a commitment to something greater than yourself.

What does this have to do with marriage? Everything. Marriage is about *human connection* at the deepest levels. In marriage, you move past the façade you show to the outside world and expose all of your raw beauty and quirky idiosyncrasies. Your mate has quirks and defects too. If you are to grow as a couple, you have to *accept* each other. To accept your mate fully you will have to be *generous* and forgive, even when those things are inconvenient. In a growing relationship you will have innumerable opportunities to be *thankful* for your mate. And together, on this great adventure of marriage, you are *committing* to something far greater than yourself.

Marriage provides you with the potential for happiness, but the way you think about marriage has a strong impact on whether you will experience it. If you think your mate is responsible for your happiness, your disappointed expectations may cause you to protect yourself and disconnect from them. If you are unable to accept your mate's differences, you will respond negatively when they surface. You will be unable to be generous with their flaws or be grateful for their positive contributions and attributes. When you have a negative mindset in your marriage you tend to hyper-focus on what's wrong and lose the ability to look beyond yourselves to something greater than yourselves.

Many couples face despair in their marriages. They see no way around the challenges they are facing and fall into harmful spirals of interaction. In most cases, these couples can rebound from their difficulties, rediscover love for their mates, and experience joy. However, some choose to end their marriages—a decision that does not ensure happiness. Most admit they never anticipated the painful consequences of terminating their union.

The way you think about marriage in these times of difficulty is critical. When my husband and I were in a profoundly difficult season of our marriage, we remained married solely because of our commitment to something greater than ourselves. When we married, we believed we were entering something sacred, something bigger than just the two of us. Because of our belief that God loves us completely and unconditionally (while our mate can only love us imperfectly) and has promised to be at work in us and, therefore, in our marriage,[6] we have been able to endure the hard seasons.

Over time, we began to see ourselves, and each other, in the light of his generous love for us. We came to realize that his intention for us was not just to remain married but to experience the richness that comes from weathering the hard times together.

Happiness is not something you chase after. It cannot be attained. It is the fruit of an open heart and a willingness to accept the challenges of your life. If you know that God has your back and intends to bring you joy, you can be thankful while he is busy at work in ways you cannot see.

More Than You Imagined

To experience your maximum marital possibilities, two things are necessary. The first is to change how you think about marriage. If you believe your mate should make you happy, you will likely be miserable. If you see differences between you and your partner as a sign of incompatibility, you will likely turn and run. If you're confident that self-fulfillment will bring you satisfaction, you will miss the joy of a shared, mutually supportive marriage. If you value protecting your personal freedom more than learning to love, you will miss the joy of intimate connection.

The second necessity is to shift your perspective about who is to blame for the problems in your marriage. Most couples who come to marital therapy see their mate as the problem. They are often unable or unwilling to see their contributions to the issues in their marriages. They guard their positions like generals at war. Underlying their intractable stance is fear—fear of being hurt if they let their defenses down, fear of vulnerability if they admit a need for change.

The reality is most problems in marriage are cocreated. Though each spouse would prefer to blame the other, it is the dynamic of the relationship that sustains the impasse. The thinking of each, and the way they respond based on their thinking, fuels that dynamic.

When Seth and Amber entered my office their level of tension was electric. After introductions, I invited them to describe their reason for coming. With a glance, Seth deferred to Amber to describe their difficulty.

"I don't trust him," she said. "He wants me to be affectionate and playful, but the minute he doesn't get what he wants, or I say something he doesn't like, he erupts in anger. It scares me. I just want to leave."

"You're always leaving," Seth said. "You are too sensitive. If I get the least bit upset, you come unglued."

"You'd come unglued too if you could see your face," Amber replied. "It scares the kids too."

"There you go, hiding behind the kids," Seth said. "They've never complained to me."

"They wouldn't dare," Amber said.

"She's always making a big deal out of nothing," Seth said. "She's the one with the problem. She turns the kids against me."

After several weeks in therapy, it was apparent that Seth did have an anger problem. He had never hit Amber or the children, but he had verbally attacked his wife on a number of occasions. We discussed what she could do when those outbursts occurred. With a safety plan in place, we continued to work on their interactions.

It was clear that Seth blamed Amber for their difficulties. He saw her as overreactive and undermining. Amber, in turn, blamed Seth. She viewed his anger as the source of their problems.

Amber shared that she had been anxious since she was a child but had started having panic attacks four months ago. Six months ago, Seth had become demanding about having sex more frequently. Eventually, Amber moved out of the bedroom and started sleeping in the den.

"I felt guilty about that," she said, "but it seemed like the only thing I could do. There was a lot of tension and I wasn't sleeping well."

"How did you feel about that, Seth?" I asked.

"I was feeling rejected and hopeless."

"He got angry and said some pretty mean things," Amber said.

"They weren't mean," Seth said. "I was just really frustrated."

Seth was not ready to take responsibility for his comments and was feeling powerless to change the situation. I decided to introduce a shift in focus.

"If you woke up one morning and your marriage had completely changed overnight, becoming the relationship you've always hoped for," I asked him, "what is the first thing you would notice?"

"The tension would be gone. Amber would want to be close to me."

"And if you had the power to make that happen, would you want to?"

"Yeah, sure."

Seth's willingness to be involved in change was a hopeful sign.

We spent the next month exploring family history and the development of their relational patterns. Seth had come from a home with an angry, critical dad who shamed him for his lack of athletic prowess. He had developed his self-protective defense of anger early in life. When Amber withdrew from him, he felt fear and shame, which provoked his angry response.

Amber's mom had been overly anxious. She'd micromanaged many aspects of Amber's life. On one occasion, without any valid reason for concern, she was afraid Amber had been kidnapped on her way to middle school. She drove to the school, pulled her out of class, and brought her home. This and other embarrassing incidents, coupled with the chronic level of reactivity by her mother, led Amber to protect herself from charged emotional interactions.

As Seth and Amber heard each other's stories, they both began to have more compassion toward the other. Each had learned behaviors in their families that were being played out in their relationship. Amber saw how her pulling away triggered fear and shame in Seth. Seth saw how his anger set off anxiety in Amber. Over time, they were able to take responsibility for their patterns of behavior and gain tools for communicating their needs differently. The problem was no longer solely the fault of the other.

On the last day of therapy, Amber eagerly shared the results of their work. "Seth has been leaving it to me to initiate sex, and I'm finding I am more interested." She shot Seth an affectionate smile.

"I realized Amber has been anxious about a lot of things," he added. "So I wanted to relieve her of needing to feel pressured in bed. I feel bad that I made it so unsafe for her for so long. I just never made the connection between my anger and her nervousness and distrust."

"He's a good guy," Amber said, giving her husband a shoulder nudge. "I'm not sure how we lost our way, but I don't ever want to go back."

"That won't happen," Seth said. "We're different now."

■ ■ ■

Your marriage can be more fulfilling than you ever imagined if you have the courage to face the ways you contribute to the difficulties and rethink some of your assumptions. Seth and Amber came to realize the patterns that were destroying their relationship. They recognized that their marriage was not just about meeting their personal needs. Using the skills discussed in chapters 4–9, they were able to move toward each other with more compassion and meet one another's needs in ways they could not have anticipated. They began to think differently about their relationship.

To have a great marriage, you have to be an outlier. You can't buy in to the cultural norm that says commitment is to be avoided because it narrows your options and you need to keep them open. That thinking will never provide the security necessary for a vulnerable, intimate relationship.

Nor can you assume that your mate should make you happy—and if they don't, it's okay to leave. That mindset will put you on a path of numerous superficial relationships.

The Bible has an interesting take on marriage. It refers to marriage as a passionate love adventure where two self-centered people (that would be all of us) learn to love each other and become refined in the process.[7] In this view, marriage is an incredibly innovative way of taking two people and their relationship and creating something new.

If you let your thinking be transformed, moving from self-focused ways of relating to extraordinary ways of loving, something new and innovative may be just around the bend.

Discussion Questions: Chapter 2

Group and Couple Questions

1. Did you begin your married life as a start-up marriage or a merger marriage? What were the challenges you faced early on? Have you been able to navigate the challenges to effectively join forces?

2. The conclusion of the study "The Surprising Science of Happiness" was that although most students preferred to have the freedom to change their minds, that freedom to keep their options open left them ambivalent and dissatisfied. Once their decisions were made and options were off the table, they grew to accept and appreciate their choices and were much happier. Were you surprised by these findings? How do you think this might apply to marriage?

3. In what ways have you each had to give up some measure of independence to give priority to your relationship? What has been most difficult about giving up that independence? What do you see as a good balance of independence and connection? What does Philippians 2:3–11 say about self-fulfillment?

4. Have you and/or your spouse had to surrender or compromise any of your individual dreams to build a shared life? What have been the challenges and benefits of doing so?

5. Read 1 John 4:9–12, Philippians 4:12–13, 2 Corinthians 8:7, 1 Thessalonians 5:18, and 1 Chronicles 22:19. How do these verses suggest we can experience joy in our relationships, especially marriage? How do they urge us toward human connection, acceptance of our life and circumstances, generosity, thankfulness, and a commitment to something greater than ourselves?

For Personal Reflection

1. Do you believe your spouse is supposed to make you happy? Why or why not?

2. Did you struggle with having to give up some of your personal independence when you got married? Do you carry any resentment toward your spouse for the compromises you have had to make to give priority to your relationship?

3. Have you been viewing your marriage as a revocable contract with options to leave if your needs aren't met? If so, how do you think this view might impact the feelings of safety and trust between you?

4. Do you agree that happiness is about human connection, acceptance of your life and circumstances, generosity, thankfulness, and a commitment to something greater than yourself? How does marriage provide unique opportunities to experience each of these?

3

Why Marriage Is Worth It

The beginning of love is the will to let those we love be perfectly themselves, the resolution not to twist them to fit our own image. If in loving them we do not love what they are, but only their potential likeness to ourselves, then we do not love them: we only love the reflection of ourselves we find in them.

Thomas Merton

If you are in the throes of a difficult marital relationship, you likely have asked yourself, *Is marriage worth it?* Is all this unhappiness likely to lead to something better, or should you leave and avoid more pain? If you choose to stay, is there hope for a future with a best-friend kind of relationship? The uncertainty of what lies ahead seems to loom like a threatening storm.

Sure, married life has its benefits, but are they compelling enough to cause you to stick it out? Consider this: a study of unhappy marriages conducted by the Institute for American Values showed that there was *no evidence* unhappily married people who divorced were any better off than unhappily married people who stayed married. As a matter of fact, two-thirds of unhappily married spouses who stayed together reported that their marriages were happy five years later.[1]

Marital researcher John Gottman notes the physical benefits of married life:

> Numerous research projects show that happily married couples have a far lower rate for physical problems such as high blood pressure, heart disease, anxiety, depression, psychosis, addictions, etc. and live four years longer than people who end their marriages.[2]

What's more, according to a national study, more than three-fifths of divorced Americans say they wish they or their spouses had worked harder to save their marriages.[3]

Impressive findings. But do they answer the question of why *your* marriage might be worth the effort? Why should you invest your energy, emotions, and time in an endeavor that seems to be more depleting than enlivening? Why hang in there "for better or for worse"? Why should you choose to endure with no foreseeable promise of relief? It's an important question that deserves serious reflection.

The reality is marriage is hard. There's no play-by-play manual and there are no days off. At its worst it is the most challenging relationship you can have, and at its best it is the most profoundly gratifying experience of your life. It will expose your deepest wounds and demand your utmost selflessness. It will surface your protective defenses and invite you to reveal your most tender vulnerabilities. It is not equal or fair but an ever-shifting seesaw of give-and-take.

There is no scorecard to measure how you're doing. There is no insurance you can buy to compensate you for the emotional capital you invest and no umbrella policy to protect you from losses. Marriage provides you and your spouse with the opportunity to see each other at your best and at your worst. And for that reason, it is the one relationship in life that gives you the greatest opportunity to grow into a person who loves well and is loved, warts and all.

One Sure Thing

Life is messy and unpredictable. Just when you think you have everything in hand, something happens: your spouse loses their job, a parent gets cancer, a longtime friend cuts off the relationship, a pet dies, your laptop crashes.

This generation has known its share of financial uncertainty. The Great Recession upended confidence that the "American Dream" was attainable. Many twenty- and thirtysomethings were stunned to discover that the economic opportunities available to college graduates in the two previous generations were not as available for them. On the contrary, unemployment soared, reaching its peak in the first decade of this century, leaving many unable to find work, buried in college debt, and financially dependent on their parents.

Many millennials have entered my office feeling lost and deceived. They had understood that these would be the best years of their lives but were struggling to find their place in the world. They had no idea what career to pursue, where they would live, or how long they would have to wait until they found a meaningful lifelong relationship. They felt uncertain about finding that special someone and even more unsure about the prospects of sustaining a fulfilling marriage. All this uncertainty translated to anxiety about the future.

Young adults are not alone in this. Our culture promotes a concept of success that includes material wealth, high achievement, and intense, passionate relationships. If you are not experiencing these, you can feel anxious—that you're not measuring up, that you're not "good enough." According to the National Institute of Mental Health, anxiety disorders affect 18.1 percent of adults in the United States (approximately forty million people between the ages of eighteen and fifty-four). If estimates include those who don't seek help, are misdiagnosed, or don't know they have anxiety issues, the number is closer to 30 percent.[4]

Why this discussion about anxiety? Because indecision about the person to whom you are married creates anxiety.

I see this in my office daily. Couples who are committed to each other and seeking help, even if they are in high degrees of conflict when they come to me for therapy, progress much more rapidly and feel more relief than those who are entertaining the possibility of splitting up. Having settled the matter of permanency, they are free to invest their energy in repair, growth, and building a future together. When you are in a relationship for the long run, you have less anxiety and can bring your undivided self to work on the marriage.

When Jill and Steve entered my therapy office, they had hit a rough patch. She was feeling emotionally distant from him and reconsidering her commitment to him. Steve had been unemployed for ten months and felt somewhat depressed. He had a hard time motivating himself and he resented the pressure he sensed from her to pound the pavement and find work. He had begun to get angry with Jill and criticize how she handled the children.

Steve struggled with anxiety. He knew he needed to accelerate his job search but found Jill's attitude crippling. His fear of her leaving left him immobilized and agitated. I asked Steve to describe how he felt physically when she talked about splitting up.

"I get tight in my chest, my stomach feels twisted, and my thoughts start racing," he said.

I then asked him if those feelings reminded him of any similar physical experience from childhood.

"Oh, yeah! When my parents would leave me at my grandparents' house for the weekend, I felt just like this. I tried sharing my fears with them, but they just dismissed my feelings and told me I'd have a great time. If I complained when we got home, my parents told me to grow up and get over it."

Steve's parents didn't know how to help him with his anxious feelings. His dad worked long hours, and although his mom stayed home, she had difficulty recognizing her own feelings, much less Steve's. When they left him with his grandparents, he felt abandoned.

After Steve recounted his story, Jill said, "I didn't realize how often Steve's parents left him. That would be hard on such a young boy."

Jill then made the connection between her distancing herself from Steve and the sense of abandonment and resulting anxiety he'd experienced earlier in life. "I had no idea that my talk about leaving felt this way to Steve. I've just been so frustrated with his lack of effort, I guess I thought threatening to split up would motivate him to get a job."

Steve leaned close to his wife. "When you first said you might leave, I thought I'd throw up. But I stuffed it. After that, I felt even more unable to make calls about jobs. And when you pushed me, I just got angry."

Jill took his hand. "I'm sorry. I was just scared. I don't know how we're going to make it financially, and it seemed like you didn't care."

Over the next two sessions, Steve and Jill began to see how their responses to each other were exacerbating their difficulties. Steve became more aware of how their financial insecurity was affecting Jill, whose parents had suffered a bankruptcy. Jill became aware of how her responses were feeding Steve's depression and anxiety.

The next session was pivotal.

After I summarized their growth from the previous two sessions, Jill turned to Steve. "I've been doing a lot of thinking. I want you to know that I am *not* leaving. I love you and we're going to work this out," she said. Steve heaved a sigh of relief. With tears in his eyes, he said, "I will do whatever it takes to find a job so you don't need to have those fears."

Steve and Jill continued to work on their relationship, intercepting negative patterns and learning to support each other in new ways. What enabled them to reignite their marital journey and gave them energy for the road ahead? The security of knowing that, in each other at least, they had one sure thing.

Castles and Moats

When there is insecurity about the future of your marriage, it is impossible to experience the safety necessary to become truly intimate partners. To reveal yourself to another, to allow your mate into your most vulnerable places, requires the assurance you will be together for the long run.

It's like we're castles, surrounded by a moat of protection to ensure that we will not be overtaken by enemy forces. When we feel safe, we let down the drawbridge, spanning the moat and allowing other people access inside. From within, our loved ones can see our vulnerabilities, our special and secret places unknown to others. They can see our weaknesses as well as our strengths.

Without the promise of fidelity and the assurance that the other person will be with you and for you forever, the risk of such intimate openness is too great. Sensing that there are conditions to the relationship puts both parties on guard. Each knows they must perform to ensure ongoing relationship and protect what could be lost if the other were to leave. The security of a steadfast partnership is necessary for us to take the risk of allowing another human being to know us at these deeper levels.

Even within the safety of a committed relationship, we can wound our mate if we are careless with the knowledge they have entrusted to us. If a confidence shared in a moment of vulnerability is used later in an argument, our drawbridge pulls up to defend against further attack. In a committed relationship, you learn to forgive and extend trust again. If your drawbridge is well oiled, it can go up and down at will. As your marriage matures over time, your drawbridge can remain lowered for longer periods of time.

When your relationship is secure, and you are committed to each other for a lifetime, you and your spouse are free to share at deeply intimate levels. Even when skirmishes surface inside the walls of your castle, you have a deep and abiding sense that you will both be there for each other, no matter what. The exclusive bond you have created relieves you of the anxiety of having to constantly guard your castle. It creates the safety required to be truly known and to fully know each other.

Becoming Best Friends

When you got married, you likely hoped your spouse would be your best friend for life. The reasons you chose your particular mate reveal what you look for in a best friend: someone who will love you no matter what, someone who will help you become the best you can be, someone you can trust with your intimate thoughts, and someone who is devoted to your well-being. Perhaps your reasons were less specific: you just couldn't imagine your life without that person or you felt an intense connection that told you, *This is the one.*

Whatever your reason for choosing your spouse, creating and sustaining a best-friend relationship requires a willingness to offer the other person room in the relationship to grow.

In every new marriage, there comes a time when both partners realize they have married someone who's imperfect. The first disappointment may be small—they don't squeeze the toothpaste right. Or it may be huge—they are addicted to pornography. Even small disappointments can lead some couples to consider calling it quits, particularly if they entered marriage with strong expectations of what their spouses needed to be for them.

The huge disappointments, particularly if they violate trust, can wreak havoc on a young marriage and cause a spouse to consider whether they married the "right" person. Whatever the severity of the infraction, whether you survive it and build a loving, lasting marriage or choose to end it depends on how willing each of you is to change and how much grace you offer each other as you both stumble toward growth.

As crazy as it may seem, we often think of ourselves as fully formed. We resist the suggestion that we have any growing to do. When a bad habit or an uncaring comment offends our spouse, we defend our behavior and blame them for being too sensitive. We don't want to face our warts, so we try to diffuse complaints by being dismissive.

Whatever the severity of the infraction, whether you survive it and build a loving, lasting marriage or choose to end it depends on how willing each of you is to change and how much grace you offer each other as you both stumble toward growth.

The truth is we all have a lot of growing to do, and marriage is the perfect place to do it. Why? Because you and your mate have promised to love each other for better or for worse. The safety created by that promise is the perfect soil in which to nurture new growth.

Each of us has a longing to be un-conditionally loved—to have some-one in this world who sees us for who we truly are and loves us still. In the presence of this person, we can be fully ourselves without pretending or performing. We know this individual loves us and we can put down our walls and defenses.

Although we desire this kind of love, we have a hard time giving it. If we are honest with ourselves, we don't want to provide such love to another person. To love someone unconditionally, without requiring something in return, is beyond our human capacity. We do, however, want someone to be unconditionally committed to us. That's because unconditional love is freeing. It is also comforting and transformational.

At best, our ability to love our mate unconditionally will be sporadic. In the safety of committed love, our capacity is enhanced.

As we remain devoted to and accept our spouse, we offer them space to grow. We are like hosts, extending hospitality to the total person of our mate. Marriage then becomes an invitation to our spouse to grow by being receptive to who they are now and who they are becoming.[5]

Unconditional love is something we can experience in a spiritual sense. The Bible tells us that God's love for us is unconditional.[6] It is lavish, irrevocable, and complete.[7] When we feel loved like that, we are free to be totally ourselves. We don't have to measure up, be good, or toe the line. We don't have to perform, prove ourselves, or hide. We are free to be real, to become who we truly are.

God's unconditional love is always available.[8] When we feel like we're not enough, or our mate isn't enough, we can rest in knowing that we are loved. His love can fill the tank when ours runs dry.

As we come to understand the depth of God's unconditional love for us, we can learn to let go of our demands on our mate to be our sole source of love and value. As we release our grip on them, we are transformed into people who can love more unconditionally. And we free our spouse to become more fully themselves. We give them room to grow.

As we remain devoted to and accept our spouse, we offer them space to grow. We are like hosts, extending hospitality to the total person of our mate.

You may feel a bit threatened by your mate's imperfections. More than simply being inconvenient, their faults might trigger a fear that you will not get your needs met. When you fear, you tend to constrict the space necessary for your spouse to grow.

James and Amy had difficulty giving each other this room. He sometimes felt trapped by her desire for time together, which caused him to pull away. When he did, Amy's fear of being unloved caused her to pursue him more intensely. This triggered a fear in James that he was losing his independence, so he pulled further away. This pursuer-avoider pattern was driven by fear. Neither was hopeful the other could change in any significant way, which fueled their self-protective efforts.

One session highlighted this impasse.

"She's so insecure," James said. "I feel smothered by her need to spend every minute on the weekends together. I can't even play golf with my buddies anymore."

"That takes five hours!" Amy said. "That's a quarter of our weekend."

James shot a look my direction. "See? She counts the hours. I can't live like this."

"He doesn't get it." Amy's gaze dropped. "He'll never be able to give me what I need."

"And I'll never be enough for her."

Neither James nor Amy believed that the other could change. They saw in their marriage a pattern of defeat, where their needs would never be understood or met. Their mutual fear constricted the relationship. Rather than creating an open space in which each could understand the other's needs, James and Amy's responses were confining each other.

Giving your mate time and space to grow isn't easy. Offering a place where they can shed their mask and be real with you is especially difficult when your needs and desires are clamoring for attention.

Often, learning to give our mate space requires that we understand how our own wounds are getting triggered by their behavior. It also requires an awareness that our mate is not in control of our happiness. This awareness allows us to give up our demands that our mate make us happy. Eventually, if you are able to offer your spouse room to grow, space to truly be themselves, your marriage will be life-giving and you will lay the foundation for the two of you to become best friends for life.

The Stages of Married Life

If you are in a difficult season of your married life, let me assure you that, for most married couples who stick it out, life does get better! All relationships go through predictable developmental stages.[9] If you can identify the characteristics of each stage, you can begin to invest your energy in purposeful efforts that will help you transition into the next stage.

When you and your spouse first met, you likely spent a good deal of time exploring each other's interests, feelings, thoughts, and personalities. As the relationship moved forward, you missed each other when you were apart and looked forward to "us" time, when the two of you could be together. Your desire to remain independent was gradually eclipsed by your desire to be coupled.

In this *romantic* stage of the relationship, you enjoyed the experience of bonding to each other, the delight of giving to your partner and having them give to you. You saw the best in each other and experienced the joy of feeling unconditionally loved.

Looking back now, you may acknowledge that you deferred your own needs, wants, and even personality as you melded your individual lives into becoming a couple. Who you were together became more important than who you were individually.

As you entered marriage, the dream that you began to create together continued to drive your relationship. Conflict was, for the most part, avoided, as it was seen as disruptive to your shared life. Differences were downplayed and similarities were highlighted. Communication focused primarily on expectations that each of you brought to married life. These expectations directed the roles you played in your home life, work, and parenting. Expectations about how the other should be or behave were mostly silent and suggestive, not overt and directive. The dream you had for a life together gave you hope that your needs and wants would be satisfied.

The powerful connection of this early romantic stage is crucial, as it sets a foundation of trust and nurture that will be a necessary resource for future married life.[10] The dream of this stage is, however, mostly an illusion. As the bliss of romance subsides, and the reality of a married life with two real individuals surfaces, a new opportunity presents itself.

In the second stage of married life, *disillusionment*, the individual identities, personalities, priorities, and expectations of each partner reemerge and the dream is threatened. Differences, so long suppressed, begin to surface. In an attempt to eliminate these, you and/or your mate may resort to criticism, shaming, coercing, avoiding, demanding, and other forms of manipulation.

Conflict often erupts in cycles of fighting and withdrawing. Arguments escalate quickly, and communication can be hurtful and disrespectful as the two of you compete for your needs to be addressed and met. Imperfections, which remained submerged or overlooked in the joint venture of courtship and early bonding, now come to light. These imperfections, along with the painful differences that surface, create anxiety, frustration, and disillusionment.

As a result, you and/or your spouse may seek to reestablish your identities by resuming the pursuit of your unique interests, whether with others or alone. The reemergence of both individuals, though inevitable and necessary for true intimacy to be experienced, can threaten the "us" of the relationship.

One of you may reassert your identity earlier than the other, which may initiate a pursuer-distancer pattern. If both of you pull away at the same time, you may end up feeling more like roommates than lovers. Although the disruption and potential death of the dream may feel scary, this is an important step in learning to embrace the reality of intimate life with another human being.

The third stage of marriage is *rediscovery*. In this stage you have each explored and clarified your identity and can speak for yourself without demanding your partner feel and think as you do. You can each accept the flaws and differences of each other and, consequently, you can bring your authentic selves to the relationship.

Disagreements still occur, but they are void of the negative reactivity and manipulative efforts of stage 2. You are more able to de-escalate a conflict and repair the damage quickly. Communications are more respectful and productive, characterized by the freedom to express your feelings and thoughts and a willingness to listen.

Because both of you are open to the needs and wants of the other, there is a more equal balancing of roles and a sense of shared responsibility for the demands of daily life. A new sense of "us" develops that honors the value and contribution of both partners, while you enjoy a togetherness that is organic and enlivening.

You and your mate support each other's individual interests yet are mindful to balance these with ample couple time. A true interdependence emerges that allows you each to be fully yourself and fully together. In this stage, you are able to see your spouse as a person who, like yourself, is flawed and broken but in the process of becoming.[11]

Because of the growing sense of safety and warmth, sexual intimacy is reenergized. Qualitatively different from sex in stage 2, where intimate physical connection is at the mercy of conflicted emotional states, sex in stage 3 is affectionate and deeply satisfying, the reward of true friendship.

The fourth stage is characterized by a deep intimacy and friendship hewn out of the struggles and adjustments of married life. This season is characterized by a kind of *synergy* where the combined interactions of the couple have, over time, produced an effect that is greater than the sum of the individual contributions.[12]

In this stage, each of you becomes more giving and understanding. You take joy in each other's differences and support each other's development. Communication is open, genuine, and caring. Conflict is accepted as healthy, navigated without hostility, and used for growth. Roles are not an issue, as each of you contribute to benefit the whole.

As you encourage each other to become your authentic selves, your gifts and energy are released to contribute to the world and to those who come after you. In this stage you savor your shared history and enjoy the fruit of the work, love, and challenges of your married life.

■ ■ ■

Most couples make it through the first stage but get shaky during the second. In the heat of stage 2, couples typically go one of four ways:

1. They seek to reinstall the dream of stage 1, hiding and denying differences to avoid conflict.
2. They continue their escalating arguments, which become more hurtful and discouraging.
3. They exit the relationship.
4. They make room for each other's uniqueness and the differences that are an inevitable part of their ongoing relationship.

If they choose number four, the couple will reevaluate their expectations of each other and their marriage, noticing that their often unconscious and rigid expectations have stifled rather than enlivened their marriage. This shift is only possible if one or both are willing to give up the illusion of the romantic stage, recognize the damage of the manipulative efforts of the second stage, and discover the reality of life together beyond the dream. In my experience, one mate typically initiates this step, usually followed by the partner when they notice the first spouse's game-changing attitude.

Those who choose the path of divorce have difficulty imagining that their current pain and conflict can give way to something more satisfying. They are often caught in a cycle of mutual blame, struggling to extricate themselves from the overwhelming negativity.

They imagine life would be better with someone else, or at least without their spouse.

The problem with this thinking is that couples who divorce rarely move to stage 3, rediscovery, when they remarry. Most regress to stage 1, the romantic stage, and start a new dream that will likely have its eventual demise. Remarrying couples typically move more rapidly into stage 2 than those in first marriages, as they often have added stresses such as stepfamily dynamics, an ex-spouse, alimony, and/or child support.

Even without these additional challenges, many who leave their first marriages do so blaming their spouses and do not address their own contributions to the marital problems. This puts the second marriage at risk. Though you may think you are leaving your problems behind, you take yourself with you into the next relationship. This may account for the 67 percent divorce rate for remarrying couples.

However, if you accept differences and do the hard work required for intimacy to grow in your current marriage, you can shift into stage 3 and enjoy the benefits of increased intimacy, more loving communication, and deeper levels of respect and reciprocity. With less energy focused on conflict and competition over needs, you are able to enjoy each other in new ways. As time passes you slip into stage 4, where the sweetness of what you have cocreated through the years bears its greatest reward.

If you are presently in stage 2, commitment may feel more like a trap than a path to the joys of a long-term relationship. You may be afraid to stay in a marriage that takes so much effort and has such painful conflict. You may find it difficult to imagine that the hard work can produce deep levels of intimacy and joy.

In my thirty years of marriage counseling, I have helped guide hundreds of couples from stage 2 (the stage at which most husbands and wives enter therapy) to stage 3, and I have yet to meet a couple who isn't glad they put in the effort to work through their problems and enjoy the reconnection and growth that resulted.

Marriage Is Like the Stock Market

In the stock market, investors generally do best when they don't react to the day-to-day swings in stock prices.[13] Investors tend to do poorly when they look at the newspapers each morning to see if their chosen funds are doing as well as others and constantly change their investments. They move their money around so often that long-term growth is compromised, and they usually lose more money than those who keep investing whether the market is up or down.

Think of your marriage as a long-term investment. The ups and downs of satisfaction are inevitable and normal. In healthy marriages, satisfaction can be down for long periods of time only to rebound later to yield valuable dividends. If you get too focused on the down cycles, you may bail out too quickly and lose much of what you've invested. Successful couples keep investing, whether the relationship feels great or not. That's why it takes commitment—a long-term view.

Think of your marriage as a long-term investment. The ups and downs of satisfaction are inevitable and normal. In healthy marriages, satisfaction can be down for long periods of time only to rebound later to yield valuable dividends.

Are you hedging your bets? People with a short-term view of marriage scrutinize the costs and benefits of their relationship on a day-to-day basis. These people are likely to "move their investments around," looking for other places to devote their energy—work, sports, volunteering, affairs, or whatever gives them a sense of being valued. Their investments become so diverted their marriages lose momentum.

Financial experts tell us to diversify. The healthy way to do that in marriage is to multiply the number of ways you invest in the relationship. It's like having a mutual fund that includes a wide variety of stocks. In addition to sex and affection, for instance, you can develop new shared interests, volunteer together, nurture your spiritual connection, do one playful activity every week, attend a marriage retreat, and more. In all these ways, you are expanding your avenues of connection—*within* the marriage. At various times during your life, some of these avenues may not work as well as others. But by having spread your assets, you will stay connected. Regular diversified investment is the key to preventing erosion in your commitment.

Because investors with short-term views tend to get burned in the stock market, financial experts often advocate a strategy called dollar-cost averaging. In this approach, you choose a good mutual fund and stick with it. You contribute a set amount into the fund at regular intervals (e.g., $50 per month) whether the market is up or down. This strategy is very effective for beating inflation and saving something for the future.

Marriage works in much the same way. It is best if both partners are regularly investing in the relationship, whether their satisfaction level is currently up or down. You make deposits when you listen attentively, validate each other, forgive, put self-interest aside to do something that helps the other person, treat each other with kindness and respect, and so forth. Your portfolio strengthens and eventually you will enjoy the dividends of your wise investments.

■ ■ ■

Is it worth it to stay in your marriage? Is there any hope for a satisfying future with your spouse? In my experience, the answer is very probably. Every marriage has growing pains. But they also have incredible potential. Discovering the possibilities begins with reimagining what your marriage can be, staying the course, and opening yourself to new growth.

Discussion Questions: Chapter 3

Group and Couple Questions

1. Why might seeing your marriage as a sure thing create the conditions for growth in your marriage? Read John 10:11–15. How does Jesus's commitment to love us give us security?

2. Read 1 Chronicles 16:34, John 3:16, and 1 John 3:1. What do these verses say about God's love for us? How might knowing you are securely loved by God impact your ability to love in your marriage?

3. What are you doing to diversify your investments in your marriage? In what ways are you making regular deposits in your marital bank account? Exchange ideas.

4. In what stage of married life do you find yourself today—romance, disillusionment, rediscovery, or synergy? Read 2 Corinthians 3:18, 5:17, and Romans 12:2. How do these verses encourage you to know that God himself is at work helping you to grow toward more enjoyment of him and each other?

For Personal Reflection

1. Can you identify times when you have let your mate "inside your castle"? Can you identify times when you felt compelled to keep your drawbridge up, fearing your mate might see your vulnerabilities? What would need to happen to allow you to keep it lowered for more extended periods of time? Share this with your mate.

2. In what ways have you created space in your relationship for your mate to grow? In what ways have you made it unsafe for them to reveal their true self?

3. Neither James nor Amy believed that the other could change. They saw their marriage in a pattern of defeat, where their

needs would never be understood or met. Can you relate to their struggle? Have you ever allowed your disbelief in your mate's capacity to grow to confine your relationship?

4. What are you doing to diversify your investments in your marriage? In what ways are you making regular deposits in your marital bank account?

5. In what stage of married life do you find yourself today— romance, disillusionment, rediscovery, or synergy? What might you need to let go of to allow your marriage to progress to the next stage?

PART 2

Revitalizing Marriage— Changing the Way You Relate

4

Search Yourself

One of the best wedding gifts God gave you was a full-length mirror called your spouse. Had there been a card attached, it would have said, "Here's to helping you discover what you're really like!"

Gary and Betsy Ricucci

Knowing yourself is not as easy as it sounds. Most of us can identify our own preferences—a night out in the city or a quiet evening at home, a juicy steak or a salad with chicken—but understanding ourselves at deeper levels is not so obvious. We assume we know ourselves well, particularly if we're decisive and goal-oriented. We seem to know the path we're on and where we're headed. But if we look a bit closer, we each have parts of ourselves that are a bit of a mystery, even to us.

The presence of these parts is evidenced by how reactive we can be in certain situations. Your husband forgets to pick up something you'd asked him to bring home, and when he arrives without it you tear into him. Your wife expresses disappointment about not being able to afford a weekend away, and you attack her for her lack of gratefulness. If we're honest, we will admit that sometimes our reactions are far more intense than the situation warrants.

Often we will justify our reactivity and focus instead on the fault of our mate. "If he hadn't forgotten, I wouldn't have gotten so mad." "If she didn't spend so much, I wouldn't have yelled." We justify our behavior even if we have a suspicion we may have over-reacted. Both our reactivity and our justifying can be seen as parts of ourselves that jump into action when our needs are threatened.

Sometimes our responses are not so obvious to outsiders. We might be adept at keeping our emotions inside, not letting on that we are disturbed or affected. Whether our reactions are obvious or beneath the surface, they often indicate deep wounds that are not apparent to our conscious awareness.

Remember Seth and Amber? Seth's anger had been escalating in the months prior to entering therapy, but initially he was unable to acknowledge its intensity or effect. He was in denial about being angry, shifting the blame for his behavior onto Amber, whom he accused of being "too sensitive." He saw their problem as primarily Amber's. When he was willing to admit his own frustration, he traced the provocation to his wife's sexual withdrawal.

Although Amber was more aware of her increasing anxiety, surfacing in the form of panic attacks, she was unaware of its origin and felt powerless to calm it. The combination of their two reactions created a level of tension between Seth and Amber that was palpable. Without clarity about why they did what they were doing, they remained at the mercy of their destructive pattern.

Why Look Inside?

Many of us fear looking inside ourselves. We don't know what we'll find. If we've had a painful past, we prefer to leave it behind and focus on what we hope will be a more promising future.

Understanding our inner workings is not a skill we learned growing up. Instead, we learned to focus on the needs and moods of others and adapt ourselves accordingly. Wanting to be connected to our caregivers, we learned to put forward those parts of ourselves that were pleasing and accepted and hide those parts that were unwanted or needy.

Taking an inside look is, therefore, often an unfamiliar effort and not unlike starting down a road with unrecognizable terrain. You're not sure what you will discover and assume the road you're already on is just fine. It's gotten you through life to this point, so why mess with it? Besides, what if you don't like what you discover and end up feeling more shame and guilt?

At the core we long to be accepted. Many of us experienced disapproving or shaming voices as a child and have a fear that if others were to truly see us, they would confirm that we are bad or unacceptable. We fear the judgment and rejection of others, so we hide our uglier aspects and deny they exist. We are unaware that grace is available, even for our most unlovely parts.[1] But to receive that grace, we must come out of hiding.

Knowing yourself deeply and learning to acknowledge all parts of yourself is freeing. When you are able to see the ways you protect and defend yourself as parts you developed to help you manage life, you find that you are less driven by them and more able to freely admit their impact on others.[2]

You can begin to look at your reactivity and get curious about it rather than defensive. Self-exploration frees you from the endless cycle of behaving poorly and justifying it. It allows you to step back and experience a healthy separation between yourself and the ways you've learned to protect yourself.

When you are able to see the ways you protect and defend yourself as parts you developed to help you manage life, you find that you are less driven by them and more able to freely admit their impact on others.

Once you are aware and can identify these parts, you have more room inside to choose to respond rather than react. Richard Schwartz, who developed the Internal Family Systems model, is responsible for this concept of "understanding of parts," which frees you to see yourself more clearly.

As a result of this freedom, you will be able to live more authentically. Rather than living out of *shoulds* or scripts that were handed to you as a child, you will be more able to live out of your true self. As Frederick Buechner describes:

> [Our] original shimmering self gets buried so deep we hardly live out of it at all . . . rather, we learn to live out of all the other selves which we are constantly putting on and taking off like coats and hats against the world's weather.[3]

Your true, original self is who you were made to be.[4] To live authentically, then, is to discover your "original shimmering self," as reflected to you by the One who made you. It is to be open to continually learning about yourself, to have the courage to face your fears and doubts, to sort through the messages and baggage of childhood. The authentic self does not fear the judgment of others. It is content to be oneself, however imperfect. To be authentic is to engage in the process of knowing yourself deeply and living from your heart.

Another benefit to searching yourself is richer relationships. When you are free to explore yourself, you can relate to others, including your mate, in a more transparent way. As you get to know the reactive parts of yourself and why they attempt to protect you in the way that they do, you no longer need to defend them. You can appreciate these parts and know they are just *parts* of you—they do not define you. You can apologize and seek forgiveness more readily. As you relate to your mate in this less defended way, you are able to enjoy more responsive, less reactive interactions that allow for more closeness.

As you search yourself and offer yourself compassionate understanding, you are able to offer the same to your mate. Rather than judging and accusing, you can offer compassion to their wounded parts and understanding to their protectors. As you come to embrace all your parts and your true self, you are able to be more receptive to all of your mate, offering them room to be real, room to grow.

Why We Do What We Do

Human beings are born with a deep longing for unconditional love. We yearn for someone to see us completely and love us still. To be known without being loved is painful. To be rejected is wounding to the core. We desire relationships in which we can be fully known and freely loved.

We also long to feel valued—to know that we matter to someone. We want to have an impact on the world around us. Initially we discover our importance through our primary caretaker, most often our mother. As an infant, when you cried because you were hungry or needed to be changed and your mother attended to your needs, you felt comforted. Her presence, attention, and warmth helped you feel secure in the world. You mattered.

If your primary needs to feel loved and valued were not fully met, you felt pain. As a young child, you weren't able to put words to this ache but you felt it nevertheless. To cope with it, you developed protectors—ways of being that helped you manage it and avoid feeling it. Although these protectors attempt to guard us against future injury by defending us, they also work to keep our young, vulnerable parts from our awareness.[5]

If your parents were angry, you may have learned to hide your feelings and needs and accommodate their moods. If your parents were too busy for you, you may have clamored for their attention to get your needs met or learned not to need them, not to be a burden. You may have developed demanding or avoiding protectors to help you cope with an unavailable parent. If your parents were critical, you may have tried to please them to avoid their displeasure or became angry in order to defend yourself. In short, we all have developed protective parts—ways of guarding ourselves from further injury and managing life.

We carry these protectors into our adult relationships. They are like stowaways aboard the ship of our life. We don't realize they're there until they pop out of the ship's hold when we land in a relationship.

James and Amy discovered their "stowaways" when their marriage hit a rocky shore. Amy's mom had high expectations for Amy's school and chore performance and tended to micromanage her daughter's homework and extracurricular activities through high school. Amy unconsciously developed a task-oriented protector that accommodated her mom's expectations.

When she married James, that part worked hard to create an orderly home. When James disregarded her desire for tidiness, Amy became frustrated and angry. The young, vulnerable part of Amy, who feared rejection if she didn't keep a perfect house, was shielded by this protector.

Likewise, James was equally unconscious of what was driving his behavior. He minimized Amy's feelings because they seemed unreasonable to him. Growing up in a home where his feelings weren't welcome, he had learned to shield himself by becoming dismissive of his own emotions. When he married Amy, James found her desire for emotional closeness threatening. Having rarely paid attention to his own feelings, he felt inadequate to deal with hers. His avoidant protector demeaned Amy for her constant desire for his attention. James's vulnerable longing for unconditional love and attunement, so long neglected, was buried deep.

James and Amy needed to understand their protectors and the roles they were playing, as well as give attention to their wounded parts, in order to forge new relationship patterns. Toni Herbine-Blank applied Internal Family Systems to work with couples and created a "courageous communication" model that has been imminently helpful in my work to help couples change their interactions. The session in which we began to address these issues became a turning point. The tension was thick as they seated themselves in my office. James reported that the previous day, Amy had "exploded" when he informed her that the trip they had planned for the end of the month would have to be postponed due to a work obligation. As Amy listened to James's account, she crossed her arms and glared at him.

"She was so irrational," James complained. "It's not that big of a deal. We can go another time."

"Irrational?" Amy cried out. "You didn't spend *your* time making all the plans!" Her bottom lip quivered. "You just don't want to go on vacation with me."

"I didn't say that! Why can't you just be reasonable?"

"Oh, so now it's my fault?"

"I'd like to slow this down," I interjected, "so we can understand what happened." I made eye contact with Amy. "When James told you he wanted to postpone the trip, what happened inside you?"[6]

"I was hurt and disappointed," Amy said.

"Can you notice where in your body you felt that hurt and disappointment?"

"My chest tightened . . . and my heart."

"And what thoughts went through your mind?" I asked.

"I thought, 'He's doing it again. He doesn't want to be with me. He's making excuses.'"

"And what did you do or say to James?"

She shrugged. "I got mad. I told him to be honest, to admit that he doesn't really want to spend time with me." Amy sniffled. "Work is always more important to him than I am."

I turned to James. "And do you know this angry part of Amy?"

"Oh, yeah."

"And what did you notice inside when she got angry?" I asked.

"I don't know."

James hadn't had much experience tuning in to his emotions and physical reactions, since they were seldom acknowledged by his parents. Learning to do so would be a significant growth goal for him.

After a minute, James said, "I think I was feeling frustrated. Then I just went numb."

"That part of you that went numb, James," I said. "What is it afraid might happen if it didn't react in that way?"

"I think it fears I'd be overwhelmed. I wouldn't know what to do."

"Does that happen often?" I asked.

"Now that I think about it, I guess it does."

"When you felt this way, what did you say to yourself?" I asked.

James looked away. "That I'll never be enough for Amy."

"Have you ever thought that before, like you're not enough for someone?"

"Oh, yeah. My dad was really hard to please. Even when I was successful in sports, he hardly seemed to notice." James was beginning to connect with his young, wounded part that was triggering his protector.

"When you felt like you weren't enough for Amy, what did you do?"

"I left. I got in my car and took off. I just needed to go for a drive."

I checked back with Amy. "When James took off on his drive, what was going on inside you?"

"I felt hopeless and alone."

"And what did you hear yourself saying to yourself?" I asked.

"That he's never going to get it. I'm never going to have what I need."

"Have you had that feeling before?"

She dropped her gaze. "I really wanted my dad's attention. But he was gone a lot. I felt I was always waiting for him."

Helping Amy slow down and notice her feelings was the first step toward recognizing the young part of herself that longed for connection.

"Amy, what is that part of you afraid will happen if James doesn't spend time with you?"

"That I'll always be alone," Amy said, and got in touch with her deepest fear.

As we continued, Amy came to realize that one of her protectors became angry whenever she sensed James pulling away. She had been doing this ever since early childhood, when her dad was unavailable or absent and her mom was preoccupied with performance and duties. The pain of her unmet need for closeness activated her angry protector.

As we explored this connection between Amy's longing for connection and her reactivity, James saw how his withdrawing triggered an old hurt. Amy began to feel more compassion for James too. She saw how he feared not being enough for her and how he needed to feel accepted before he could reconnect with her.

Our longings for loving relationships and impact are good— they are part of the way we have been created. I've never met an individual who did not long for both. Nor have I met a person who hasn't experienced pain when those longings have gone unmet to some degree.

Because we are all imperfect, we fail to love perfectly. No human being, including your spouse and your parents, can fully meet the depth of your longing to be unconditionally loved and valued.

Even after we physically and/or emotionally separate ourselves from our parents, we still attempt to get what we need from them. But they don't hold the keys to our souls. They are fallible humans just like we are.

When our parents fail to come through for us, we often turn to our mate to fill the void. The problem is they too are wounded. Our parts want to be understood and heard but believe the only way to do so is to demand, manipulate, and shame our mate into meeting our needs. Our mate's protective parts respond in kind and both of us are left frustrated and injured.

In one sense, your protectors are well meaning. They want to keep you safe and functioning. Because they have been doing their job for so long, however, they habitually take over and interfere with the intimacy and authenticity you desire. They also fear that if the young, vulnerable parts of you were exposed, they might overwhelm you and you would be reinjured. But by keeping them in hiding, the protectors hinder their healing. What they don't understand is that your young parts have been carrying burdens that, once released, will also relieve the protectors of needing to work so hard.[7]

Your young parts long to be understood and nurtured. As you take time to get to know your protectors, appreciating their hard work and offering them compassion, they can calm down, allowing you to engage with your young parts. But sometimes these well-meaning protectors have difficulty stepping down.

In one sense, your protectors are well meaning. They want to keep you safe and functioning. Because they have been doing their job for so long, however, they habitually take over and interfere with the intimacy and authenticity you desire.

On one occasion, children were brought to Jesus.[8] His adult friends, the disciples, got upset. They thought it was an intrusion and wanted to protect Jesus from the disruption. Jesus asked them to step back and let the children come to him. He welcomed the children and blessed them. Although the disciples thought they were helping, they were actually interfering with the care Jesus sought to offer.

Your protector parts often think they know best. They can be fiercely self-reliant and fearful of standing down. They are convinced that their way is the only way you can survive. They have little confidence that your true self is capable of providing adequate protection and leadership and fail to recognize the presence of any higher power to provide safety.[9]

You can begin to calm these protectors by inviting them to trust you to care for your young parts. You can ask them to step back, assuring them that your young parts can be safe with you. And, like the children with Jesus, your young parts are also safe with God. He sees them and desires to comfort and heal them.[10] He sees you, accepts you completely, and loves you beyond your wildest imagination. As you come to understand his love for you, a space is created for all your parts to be known and cared for.[11] As you understand the fears and intentions of your protectors and lean into God's presence, your true self emerges and your protectors begin to settle.

As you are able to offer more understanding to your own parts, you can begin to relate to your spouse from a place of compassion, offering understanding to theirs as well.

Getting to Know Yourself

So how do you go about getting to know yourself? How do you gain the self-awareness necessary to live a more conscious life and have a more intimate marriage? Here are a few steps that will help you begin.

1. Check Your Dashboard

The first step in doing some healthy self-inquiry is to pay attention to your feelings. In one sense, your emotions are like the indicator lights on your car's dashboard. When they go on, there's a pretty good chance something is happening that you need to pay attention to. Your lights may have been flashing for some time, but you haven't done anything about them because you're afraid of what you might find. In order to have a well-tuned, smooth-running vehicle, you need to know what's going on under the hood. With the right amount of attention, your car will be able to go the distance.

Most of us make decisions out of a combination of our thoughts and our emotions. When it comes to big choices like where you'll live or when you'll get married, you are likely influenced by both the practical realities and how you feel. Some people, however, are so driven by their emotions they tend to react to events and other individuals rather than using a balance of feeling and thinking. Other people are so cut off from their emotions that they don't even consider feelings when they make decisions. Paying attention to how we feel and what we think, and exploring our underlying motivations, is important for anyone who wants to live a fully conscious, meaningful life.

A simple way to begin to become more self-aware is to notice feelings and thoughts that come up throughout the day. Keep a journal and record at least three emotions you experienced each day, along with the physical reactions and the thoughts that coincided with each feeling. Here's an example:

What happened: I walked into a business meeting today.
Feeling: Anxiety.
Physical reaction: My hands were jittery and my stomach was clenched.
Thought: This presentation had better be good. My last one wasn't as sharp as it could've been.

Here's another example:

What happened: Jack came home from school today with a note from the teacher that he didn't turn in an assignment.
Feelings: Anger and embarrassment.
Physical reaction: My shoulders were tight and my cheeks were flushed.
Thought: The teacher will think I'm a bad parent.

Use the "Feeling Words" list in appendix A to help you describe your emotions.

2. Explore Your Upbringing

Understanding the impact of how you were raised can help you gain clarity about how you relate to others—in particular, your spouse. How was conflict handled in your home? Were you allowed to express feelings? If so, which ones? Did you have parents who provided tender emotional comfort when you were hurting? Or were you expected to buck up and dismiss your feelings?

An honest look at the good and bad of your upbringing will allow you to see what is true about yourself and your circumstances. Then you can avoid the black-and-white thinking that causes you to lay full blame on your parents or yourself.

Amy was initially resistant to seeing her anger toward James as unreasonable. When she considered the impact of her dad's absence and her mom's anxiety that drove her focus on performance, she realized how she had depended on James to repair the wounds of her childhood. As she became more conscious of the fears and longings that drove her behavior, she was able to have compassion for her wounded parts that triggered her anger. She was then able to free James from the weight of her unmet needs. When he no longer felt diminished by her demands and criticism, he could comfort her.

Since Amy no longer felt dependent on her parents for validation of her worth, she experienced a more adult relationship with them. She could love them without demanding something in return. And she set boundaries with her mom's anxious expectations.

Whatever your upbringing, or your responses to it, doing some serious introspection about the dynamics of your home and the impact it has had on how you engage in intimate relationships is imperative to enjoying the warm, healthy, long-lasting marriage you desire. Here are some questions that can help you begin your exploration.

1. Do you have clear memories of your childhood? If you have very few childhood memories, this likely indicates you have a protector that disconnects you from painful memories for fear you will be overwhelmed or invalidated if you actually felt them. If this is true, ask your siblings or others who knew you as a child about the realities of your early home life.

2. Do you have memories of being listened to and warmly affirmed by a parent? Think of specific instances that were significant to you. Did such attunement characterize the way your parent was with you throughout childhood, or was it limited to one or two notable instances?

3. How were feelings expressed in your family? Were they openly shared or dismissed and invalidated? Were your parents uncomfortable expressing their own feelings? Which feelings were allowed and which were not? Did you have a moody or emotionally unpredictable parent? What did you typically do with your own feelings as a child?

4. What were your most significant childhood disappointments? What did you long for that you did not receive? Can you think of specific instances of hoping for some kind of emotional connection that did not happen or for affirmation that was not forthcoming?

5. Were your parents critical or overprotective? Did you find yourself yearning for their approval or trying to be very good? Did you feel anxious when your parent left or returned? Were they often unavailable or too involved? How did that make you feel?

6. What were your parents' expectations of you? Did you strive to meet them? Did you feel like a disappointment to your parents? If so, what did you do with the pain of feeling you had let them down?

7. As you think about the hurts or disappointments in your marriage, can you trace them back to any wounds from childhood? What topics or activities are you particularly

sensitive about? What does your spouse do or say that stirs the strongest reaction in you? Can you think of anything from childhood that triggered a similar reaction?

8. Did you have the experience of parents who divorced? If so, what feelings did you have about it? How were you told? How did your parents talk about the divorce? How did they talk about one another? Did they invite you to talk about your feelings and offer comfort or just expect you to adapt?

9. Did you grow up in a home where there was violence, abuse, alcoholism, or mental illness? How did family members respond? Was anyone safe or protective of you? Did they deny there was a problem or try to cover it up? Did they expect you to keep family secrets? How did you cope with the unpredictability of your environment?

As you consider your upbringing, try to notice the feelings you had as a child. Were you sad, angry, confused, or scared? Or were you numb, disconnected, or anxious? Your emotions can give you clues as to what protectors you may have developed to cope with your circumstances.

If you have difficulty identifying any feelings, chances are you may have a "disconnector" part that avoids, dismisses, and shuts down. That often happens when our feelings were disregarded or punished in childhood.

3. Identify Your Protectors

In addition to considering your upbringing, one of the best ways to identify your protectors is to notice your reactions in conflict. That's because we usually react to threats by using patterns of protecting ourselves that we learned in childhood. Some protectors are reactive—they jump in to make sure we aren't hurt again. Some protectors are preemptive—they attempt to manage situations so we won't be exposed to pain.[12]

Protectors come in all shapes and sizes. Here are some examples of protectors and their purposes:

- *Anger* is usually an attempt to compel others to meet our need for respect or attention or get them to back off.
- *Withdrawal* ensures that others can't get close enough to hurt us. It also can protect us from being exposed as somehow deficient.
- *Joking* can keep others at a distance through humor and keep the conversation light so as to not touch on anything too deep or painful.
- *Analyzing* allows us to assess situations in advance so we aren't taken by surprise. It allows us to distance ourselves and feel in control.
- *Judging* places condemnation on someone else as a way of feeling superior and invulnerable, or on ourselves in order to deflect attention from the wounded parts of our hearts.

Most people have any number of protectors. For a more comprehensive list of possible protectors, see appendix B.

■ ■ ■

Take some time to assess how you responded in a recent conflict with your spouse. Use the following questions to help in your exploration.[13]

1. What happened? What did your spouse say or do that triggered a reaction in you?
2. What emotion came up in you when it first happened? Did other emotions follow? (Use the "Feeling Words" list in appendix A.)
3. What was the first thought that came to your mind? Did other thoughts follow? For example, *I want to leave. I'm unimportant. I'm right. Why can't my partner . . . ?*

4. What did you want to do immediately?

5. What did you actually say or do?

6. How did your partner respond?

7. What did you feel, think, and do when they responded in that way?

8. Can you identify a common pattern in your interactions?

9. What do you typically do to protect yourself when you get into these patterns?

10. Do your feelings remind you of a time in your childhood when you felt compelled to protect yourself in a similar way?

Your emotions, reactions, and self-protective efforts help you identify your protectors. Once you have done so, you might want to interview them.[14] Ask each of your protectors what they believe their role to be and what they fear might happen if they didn't jump in to protect you. Ask them how long they've been doing their job and if they are aware of the young part that they have been trying to protect all this time. You might also ask how old they think you are (they often think you are quite young and still in need of their vigilant protection). It can be helpful to write out your answers.

Let your protectors know how much you appreciate their hard work for you and invite them to notice that you are an adult now. You have a voice and can speak on your own behalf. Ask them to trust you to see your young, vulnerable parts and care for them. Invite them to notice that God is trustworthy to care for your young parts as well.

Extend compassion to both your protectors and your young parts. Over time, as you are able to notice and reassure your protectors that you are present and your young parts that they are loved and safe, your internal system will calm. Your parts will be less inclined to jump in and hijack you, and you will be able to respond to your spouse with less reactivity.

Identifying the feelings you had in childhood and the adaptive protectors you may have developed is beneficial for several reasons. It gives you clarity about the origins of your way of relating. It also helps you develop compassion for yourself. As you learn about what has contributed to any hurtful habits you may have developed, you will be less inclined to shame yourself, more able to acknowledge the hurt and seek forgiveness, and more empowered to make new choices in the future. Remember, your protectors developed to help you cope and believe they are still helping. Understanding them and extending compassion to them can free you to be less defensive and more self-aware.

You can also develop more compassion for your mate, who also has had formative negative experiences. Each of you can begin to identify your own patterns and make new choices about how to relate. You may find it helpful to engage the support and expertise of a good therapist to help you explore the impact of your past and assist you in making connections to your present style of relating.

4. Invite Feedback

Ask others, including your spouse, to give you candid feedback about how you come across. This is a courageous thing to do, as the input may be difficult to hear. But it can reap meaningful rewards.

The relationships in our lives can be like a mirror reflecting us to ourselves and revealing how we relate to others. Marriage provides innumerable opportunities for such awareness. It exposes our patterns and protectors like no other relationship.

If we lived on a deserted island, we would have no need to develop as human beings. But we live with the daily challenge of relating to others who are different from us. And with our mate, we live in close proximity to someone who is privy to our harmful patterns and selfishness. We can either defend ourselves against their observations or allow ourselves to be refined by the challenge of intimate relating.

We are often blissfully unaware of our inner workings and our impact on those around us. Remember Steve and Jill? Jill had been unaware of how her nagging Steve to find work affected his anxiety. When she discovered how paralyzing her efforts to motivate her husband were, she asked Steve to tell her about other ways her behavior was activating his anxious protector.

Then Steve thought about how his difficulty searching for work was affecting his wife's sense of security. He invited Jill to share what went on inside her when he became immobilized in his job quest and when he deflected her concerns. This exploration led to an understanding of their protectors and the cycle of mutual activation. Soon they were discussing how they could both participate in calming their reactivity.

Asking your mate for feedback is humbling and connecting. It tells them you want to grow and learn to love better. Inviting trusted others who know you well to share their perceptions of you, while being non-defensive and fully receptive, can give you rich information that leads to positive change. It can also strengthen those friendships and inspire them to invite feedback as well. As a result, you will enjoy deeper and more authentic relationships that bring you joy and meaning.

5. Create Soul Space

Life can be crazy hectic. So many of the young moms I speak with are overwhelmed with all that is on their plate and desperate for some time to themselves—time to think, rest, and just be. Although some downtime sounds nice, the idea of having to make all the plans necessary to enjoy it—babysitters, food preparation, reservations, laundry, and so forth—make even a small getaway a huge effort. Husbands and dads are stressed as well. Striving to prove themselves in the workplace while managing their family responsibilities can leave them with little margin for much else.

We are so used to running so fast that, if and when we finally slow down, the quiet can be quite disturbing. It's amazing how used to constant stimulation we can become. One young husband recently disclosed to me that he can't go to sleep unless the television is on. Quiet creates anxiety for him. The steady drone of noise is somehow reassuring.

Our need to be constantly connected on Facebook, Twitter, Snapchat, Instagram, and other social media sites makes us worry if we go for a few hours without checking our phone. Are we just social animals or do we fear missing out? Do we fear being alone? Is the constant connection itself a protector that guards us from feeling unloved or unimportant?[15]

Alone time can restore our sense of peace in the midst of all the pushes and pulls of life, or it can throw us into anxiety. Busyness can be one of our most go-to protectors, as it keeps us from looking inward and, like all protectors, pushes away what we don't want to see. Some of us are so afraid to slow down and take an inside look that we stoke the raging fire of busyness so we can avoid it. The pull of fretful living is seductive as it numbs us to our insecurities, fears, and doubts.

Some of us are so afraid to slow down and take an inside look that we stoke the raging fire of busyness so we can avoid it.

We even pride ourselves on how busy and connected we can be.

Sometimes our protectors have been so active that we fear we might not like what we will find if we slow down and take an inside look. Not only are we concerned that our pain or fears might overtake us but we even fear that at the core we are empty—that there's not much there. This is untrue.

At your center, you are a beautiful self. If you don't believe it, will you trust the One who made you? God says you are made "in his own image" (Gen. 1:27). Your true self reflects his very nature—compassionate, caring, creative, peaceful, loving, just, kind. Your protective parts can take over and eclipse that image but never erase it. God considers you worthy of his love and pursues you in order to restore your likeness to himself.[16]

Our protectors urge us to rely on them and remain independent of God. They have wooed us with false promises of finding life apart from him.[17] But they cannot satisfy what our hearts yearn for. Our selves are hungry for God. As God offers us relationship with himself, we can ask him for forgiveness for relying on our protectors and relinquishing control to them.

We can never have a more meaningful life or intimate relationships unless we are willing to slow down and take an inside look. Learning to nourish our spiritual life while responding to everyday demands and duties is a challenge, but it brings a beautiful balance and health to our lives. This is more than finding our purpose in life, although that too is enhanced by taking quiet times of reflection. Creating soul space is about finding a rhythm in your day, week, month, and year that includes time for spiritual nurture.

Our true self is dependent on God for life and nourishment. We need a continual inpouring of his love and time in his presence to see our way clear and sustain our connection with our "shimmering self." Psalm 36:9, referring to God, says, "In your light we see light." By spending time with him, we can begin to see ourselves, our spouse, life, and love from his perspective. This time gives us clarity and feeds our souls. It also allows us to remain keenly aware of our protectors and not be overtaken by them.

To begin, you might set aside five to ten minutes a day to be alone with God. You can use the time to simply pray, reflect, or read. There are many mobile applications that might help guide you—for example, Examine is a simple app that will help you reflect on a few thoughtful questions each day, while YouVersion offers a Bible verse to read each day and reading plans.

Prayer is an important part of this soul nurture. Your self will be strengthened by routinely thinking about and reveling in its identity as a beloved, forgiven, and delighted-in child of God while in his presence. Enjoy him, thank him, and invite him to search you and reveal to you any protectors that might be interfering with your ability to love well.

It's not uncommon for your protectors to get riled up when you begin. You may feel a desperate urge to get busy and disparage the practice as a waste of time. Hang in there. Reassure your protectors you can handle whatever may come up. Any new behavior takes time to settle into a rhythm. As you become more comfortable with solitude and more attentive to God's presence, you will enjoy a peace that permeates your day with a lightness and sense of purpose. Even a bit more patience with the kids!

Additionally, you might set aside more extended time to do one or more of the exercises in the "For Personal Reflection" section at the end of the chapter.

■ ■ ■

We sometimes have the idea that life is what happens to us. But as Carl Jung is purported to have stated, "Until you make the unconscious conscious, it will direct your life and you will call it fate."[18]

We are all directed by forces from our childhood. We choose whether or not to become conscious of them. If we don't, those forces will continue to impact our relationships with our spouse, our children, and others. If we choose the more difficult path of becoming self-aware, we can make new choices about our future.

It's hard to give up our protective patterns. They have allowed us to avoid pain. And messing with our normal way of relating is risky. We don't know what lies ahead. Without self-knowledge, however, you cannot be free to make choices and grow. You will always remain a slave to your triggers and wounds and their resulting reactivity.

Find the courage to dive in and discover the beauty of your authentic self. This is the first step toward enjoying a truly intimate relationship with your mate.

Discussion Questions: Chapter 4

Group and Couple Questions

1. How do you respond to the idea of searching yourself? Have you ever found yourself thinking:

    a) *Why should I search myself when my spouse is really the problem?*

    b) *I already feel bad about myself. Why make it worse?*

    c) *I have a painful past, and I don't want to relive it. I want to put it behind me.*

    d) *I don't want to blame my parents.*

    e) *Focusing on myself is selfish.*

    Why might exploring yourself be beneficial? Read Proverbs 20:5 and Psalm 139:23–24. What do these verses say about self-exploration and allowing God to search you?

2. Would you agree that everyone has a deep desire to be completely known and fully loved? Have you ever had the experience of being loved but not truly known? Have you ever had the experience of being known but rejected? How did these experiences make you feel? Read Psalm 139:1–4 and 1 John 4:16. What difference does it make to you to know that God knows and loves you completely?

3. As you read about the therapy session with James and Amy, could you identify with the way their mutual responses were triggering each other? Do you notice interactions with your partner in which you seem to be setting one another off? Have you ever wondered why you react as you do? Read Romans 7:15–8:2. Can you relate to Paul's struggle? How did he find rest in his dilemma?

4. Are you able to identify one or two of your "go-to" protectors—ones that predictably surface in an argument with your mate? Do you have any memory of having a similar

reaction in childhood? If you have that awareness and feel comfortable, share what you notice about yourself with your group. (Hopefully, you've established an agreement with the group to honor the confidentiality of each person. Doing so will make the sharing much more honest and helpful for all.)

5. Read Matthew 19:13–14. How do you think Jesus sees the young, vulnerable, or wounded parts of yourself? Read Luke 4:16–21 and Isaiah 66:13. What is God's heart toward restoring brokenness?

6. Commit to one another to work through the exercises in the "For Personal Reflection" section below. As you do, take time in subsequent meetings to share what you are learning.

For Personal Reflection

1. Thoughts and Feelings Exercise
   A simple way to begin to become more self-aware is to notice feelings and thoughts that come up throughout the day. Keep a journal and record at least three emotions you experience each day, along with the physical reactions and the thoughts that coincide with each feeling (see examples in the chapter).
   Use the "Feeling Words" list in appendix A to help you describe your emotions.

2. Exploring Your Upbringing Exercise
   Whatever your upbringing, or your responses to it, do some thoughtful introspection about the dynamics of your home and the impact it has had on how you engage in intimate relationships. Questions are provided in the chapter.

3. Identify Your Protectors Exercise
   Take some time to assess how you responded in a recent conflict with your spouse. Use the questions in the "Identify Your Protectors" section to help in your exploration. Most people

have any number of protectors. For a more comprehensive list of possible "protectors," see appendix B.

4. Inviting Feedback Exercise

   Invite others, including your spouse, to give you candid feedback about how you come across. Before you approach them, check in with your protectors and see if they have any concerns about doing this. See if you can reassure them and ask them to step back and allow you to ask for feedback in an openhearted way.

5. Creating Soul Space Exercise

   Set aside five to ten minutes a day to be alone with God. You can use the time to simply pray, reflect, or read. There are many mobile applications that might help guide you. Examine is a simple app that will help you reflect on a few thoughtful questions each day, and YouVersion offers a Bible verse to read each day and also reading plans.

For Further Self-Exploration

To continue exploring your upbringing and its impact on how you relate, you might take the "Love Style Quiz" on the *How We Love* website (www.howwelove.com). I would also recommend picking up a copy of *How We Love* by Milan and Kay Yerkovich to familiarize yourself with your individual love style and your combined couple style. Use the workbook section to deepen your self-awareness.

5

Embrace Differences

You come to love not by finding the right person, but by seeing an imperfect person perfectly.

Sam Keen

Stacey is organized and determined. She is very detail-oriented and thorough in both her work and personal life. But details elude Matt, her husband. He tends to be a big-picture kind of guy and leaves the details and follow-through to others. Stacey gets frustrated with how Matt habitually "forgets" to complete a task and expects her to pick up the slack.

James is matter-of-fact and analytical. He enjoys a good argument, as long as emotions are tamed and reasoning remains "logical." Amy, his wife, is much more attuned to people's feelings and tries to avoid arguments. When she is hurt, she tends to reason from her feelings. This causes James frustration, so he shuts down, becoming judgmental and distant.

Both of these couples are coping with the challenge of differences within their marriage. Although their dissimilarities may have initially attracted each to the other, over time these differences can affect how the couple experiences emotional support, trust, connection, and intimacy.

To be able to embrace differences, we will need to explore what they are, why they challenge a marriage, and how celebrating them can be beneficial to a growing relationship.

Types of Differences

You and your mate are different for many reasons. For one, as we spoke about earlier, you each had a different childhood upbringing, which powerfully impacts how you do relationship.

Consider James and Amy. James grew up in a home with disengaged parents who disparaged feelings. He learned to disconnect from his emotions and, as a result, felt overwhelmed by his wife's longing for connection. Amy grew up in a home where Dad was unavailable and Mom was physically but not emotionally present. Due to her unmet longing for closeness, she felt abandoned by James's lack of attention. In addition, James grew up in a cluttered, chaotic home while Amy's was rigidly organized. As a result, each had differing expectations for how their home would be managed.

Personality differences add another dimension to navigating your marriage relationship. Sean is energetic and outgoing. He engages easily in conversation with friends and strangers alike. His wife, Michelle, is quite a bit more introverted. She enjoys time alone and finds it more challenging to talk, even with friends, for any length of time. When they attend parties together, she is usually left to fend for herself and resents the time Sean spends connecting with others.

One of you may be more active and playful while the other may be more serious and conscientious. One of you may be more driven while the other may be more creative and thoughtful.

Physical Differences

Do you ever wonder why your wife tends to talk a lot more than you do? Or why your husband avoids lengthy or emotional conversations? That's because the male brain is different from the female brain. An understanding of these fascinating differences can help each partner be receptive to the unique design of the other.

Females possess a greater density of neurons in the parts of the temporal lobe associated with language processing and comprehension. The hippocampus, the part of the brain responsible for memory and emotion formation, is larger in the female brain, as is the brain circuitry for language and observing emotions in others.[1] As a result, girls tend to develop language faster and more comprehensively than boys. This not only accounts for a woman's tendency to be more verbal but explains her social attunement and ability to remember emotional conversations.

Males, on the other hand, perform tasks from their left hemisphere, which is the rational/logical side of the brain. Their language development occurs only in the left hemisphere of the brain. As a result, men tend to be more focused in their communication, to get right to the issue.

Our differing brain structures also explain why women can give attention to several things at once and men tend to be more singularly focused. The corpus callosum (the band of neurons that connect the left and right sides of the brain) allows both sides of the brain to work in a coordinated fashion. The larger corpus callosum in women has been proposed as a reason why women are usually better than men at multitasking. It allows for more connectivity between the left and right sides of the brain.[2] The female brain can gather more information and pick up details through their senses.

If your husband appears to have "selective attention" and doesn't hear you when he is tuned in to something else, his more focused brain is very likely the reason. Males have more connectivity *within* each hemisphere of the brain, which allows them to be more compartmentalized. They are also better at spatial processing and coordinated action.[3] Louann Brizendine, in her book *The Female Brain*, also notes that "Men have larger processors in the core of the most primitive area of the brain, which registers fear and triggers aggression—the amygdala. This is why some men can go from 'zero to a fistfight' in seconds."[4] Both coordinated action and response to threat are important to protection and survival.

Have you ever wondered why, when it comes to sex, men are more visually stimulated? The hypothalamus, located deep in the center of the brain, monitors many activities such as hunger, thirst, sex, and sleep. The pre-optic area of the hypothalamus, which is the area of the brain most involved in sexual and mating behaviors, is 2.2 times larger in men than women and has twice the number of cells. Men also have over ten times the amount of testosterone as women, which accounts for the fact that they think about sex more often. Brizendine comments,

> Just as women have an eight-lane superhighway for processing emotion while men have a small country road, men have O'Hare Airport as a hub for processing thoughts about sex whereas women have the airfield nearby that lands small and private planes.[5]

Understanding these differences in the human brain can be very useful in responding to your spouse. If a husband appreciates his wife's need to talk and connect verbally, he can make an extra effort to give her his undivided attention. In order to ensure she has her husband's full attention, a wife can be thoughtful about choosing her timing. She can also be sensitive to whether or not her husband is feeling verbally overwhelmed and adjust her conversation accordingly.

A wife who understands that men's brains are *designed* to be more focused on sex can be more accepting of her husband's sexual desire and no longer disparage him for what comes naturally. If she acknowledges her capacity for multitasking, she can choose to give the sexual experience her undivided focus. She may choose to set aside some of the tasks and responsibilities that are clamoring for her attention so she can feel relaxed and present with her husband and allow herself to enjoy sexual intimacy.

Knowing his wife may have difficulty turning off the demands of her day in order to be available for intimacy, a savvy husband can offer to help, plan romantic moments, and express his love both in and, even more importantly, outside the bedroom.

Emotional Differences

Women and men also appear to differ in their emotional needs.[6] What a wife seems to want most from her husband is his time, attention, and support. She longs for her husband's wholehearted devotion and attunement. She wants her husband to bring strength to their family without harshness or domination. She yearns to feel cared for and validated. Above all, she longs to be loved, tenderly and consistently.

Men, on the other hand, desire respect even more than love. Respect conveys to a man that he is seen as competent and capable, that he is "enough" for his wife. Expressions of disappointment pierce him like a sword. He longs to make his wife happy, to be admired and appreciated. He needs confirmation that his contributions are valuable and noticed.

When a husband and wife understand their different emotional needs, they can offer what the other truly desires—rather than what they *think* the other wants.

The Emergence of Differences

In the early romantic and idealized stage of relationship, our brain is saturated with feel-good chemicals—such as dopamine, adrenaline, and norepinephrine—that give us that heart-thumping, euphoric experience of being in love.[7] The falling-in-love experience is one in which our brain is literally "drugged." In this state, our awareness is narrowed. In our desire to connect and please, our partner's flaws and differentness are overlooked, and what is similar captures our attention.

In a few months or years, that high usually wears off. You wake up married to a "stranger" with deficiencies and annoying habits. Your husband's closeness to his mother, once sweet, becomes a painful source of contention. Your wife's attention to detail, once helpful, becomes irritating and feels overbearing.

When the different habits, needs, and perspectives of your mate, which initially attracted you to each other, become difficult and painful, you may see them as a threat to the relationship—things that must be eradicated or at least suppressed. So you try to convince your spouse to think or act differently. When that doesn't work, you resort to manipulation, perhaps shaming or criticizing them for their positions or habits. You may withdraw something they long for—such as sexual connection, time, or attention—in order to get them to change.

When the different habits, needs, and perspectives of your mate, which initially attracted you to each other, become difficult and painful, you may see them as a threat to the relationship—things that must be eradicated or at least suppressed.

But being surprised by traits, behaviors, habits, thoughts, and reactions of your mate is completely normal. When the high of falling in love subsides, the reality of being married to a real person with needs that are different from yours is inevitable. You can protest, punish, or manipulate in an effort to eliminate the differences between you, but that will only further wound your mate and harm your marriage.

It may be that your response to the annoying or painful differences of your mate is being driven by an unconscious desire to repair a wound from childhood. If you are highly reactive or avoidant as a way of dealing with your mate, this is very likely true. If you are hoping to find, in your mate, that one person who could finally come through for you to meet your needs for love and value, the disappointment can be immense. Releasing your spouse from the obligation to make up for your childhood losses can be a huge turning point for you and your marriage.

Unconscious desires were definitely at work when James and Amy fell in love. He was drawn to her emotional energy and heartfelt expressions of affection. When she pursued him, his parched emotional upbringing received streams of healing water. He had finally found a woman who gave him the attention and connection he had yearned for.

Having lived with her mother's weighty expectations and obsessive cleanliness, Amy was drawn to James's relaxed nature and sense of adventure. When she would get anxious or flustered, he would help her get perspective and become calm. She was entertained by his messy apartment, and although she was confident she could help him become more organized, she appreciated his hang-loose attitude. When James would plan playful dates, Amy felt very loved.

The unconscious drives that led them to marry also played a role in their early disappointments and conflict. After the first year of marriage, the qualities they once found endearing and attractive became a source of pain. James's relaxed attitude began to annoy Amy as she tripped over his dirty clothes on the bedroom floor. Her emotional expressiveness began to create a great deal of discomfort for James. As his attentions were diverted to the increased demands of his work, Amy felt the sting of her father's unpredictable involvement in her life. When she reacted with emotional outbursts, James felt overwhelmed and frustrated. The emotional desert of his upbringing hadn't prepared him for the flood of feelings flowing from Amy. Feeling ill-equipped to handle the situation, he blamed her and withdrew.

Like most couples, James and Amy initially tried to get the other to change. Their efforts played out in our fifth session of therapy.

Amy, shifting toward the edge of the sofa, railed. "I don't get why it's so hard to throw your dirty clothes into the basket. It would take two seconds!"

"I just forget." James shrugged. "I'm in a hurry in the morning."

She turned to me. "I'm not asking that much! How can he be so lazy?"

James grimaced. "Why can't you just let it go? Is it really that big of a deal?"

I encouraged James and Amy to slow down their interaction and look at the feelings underlying their positions. Amy revealed that she felt unimportant and anxious when James would toss his clothes on the floor. The maternal part of her wanted to teach him to behave better, and the judgmental part wanted to prove him wrong. In turn James felt managed and criticized. The adolescent part of him wanted "Mom" to back off. As each was able to see their vulnerable and protective parts that were getting activated, they were able to take responsibility for their responses and have a very different conversation.

Amy moved an inch closer to James. "I'm sorry I'm on your case so much about this. Sometimes I just don't feel you hear me or that you care."

"I can see how you would feel that way," he said. "Because of our family upbringings, we have different expectations for how tidy the house needs to be."

"I know the mess doesn't bother you," Amy said, "but it grates at me because of the way I was raised."

"I don't mean to disregard you. I really just don't think about it."

"I wonder if there is a way to meet both our needs."

"I could use something visual to help me remember," James offered. "How about if we pull the basket out of the closet and put it at the end of the bed where I'll see it?"

Amy agreed, obviously encouraged by James's willingness to make an effort.

Once they were both willing to recognize that their perspective was not the only right way, they were able to listen and be heard. The focus shifted from trying to change their mate to communicating their own feelings and needs respectfully.

Different by Design

Have you ever thought of what life would be like if you were married to someone exactly like you—same background, thoughts, strengths and weaknesses, experiences, gender—in other words, you? Boring, right? Most of us marry someone who complements us, someone whose personality and giftedness completes what we lack.

My husband is an analytical thinker. I am more relational. He solves our computer problems. I connect us to friends.

If God designed marriage to be a union of two similar people, I doubt he would have made them male and female or created the multiplicity of personalities that exist. It appears much more likely that he designed marriage to be the union of two individuals with significant differences that would require a "working out" through the challenges of married life.

So, if there is purpose to your differentness, what could it be? I can think of several possibilities.

Differences Help Us See That Our Way Is Not the Only Way

You and your spouse come from different family backgrounds. It is likely that you have different views of how much time to spend with your extended families, where to spend the holidays, how much to disclose to family members, how much money to save or spend, and how to raise children. You can choose to view your mate's view as wrong, inferior, or informative. The latter choice opens you to new input and a happier marriage.

You probably even have opposing views of how thoroughly a task needs to be done. I grew up in a home where my dad had one right way to do any household chore. When my husband and I were first married, he sweetly volunteered to sweep our small patio. Little did he know that I was an *expert* patio sweeper, the keeper of the *one way* anyone should sweep a patio! I thought he would benefit from my coaching, but that did not go over well. He tossed the broom and left the chore to the "expert." We both had our own concepts of what a swept patio looked like from our past experiences. It took me several years to realize my way was not necessarily the right way or the only way.

You can choose to view your mate's view as wrong, inferior, or informative.

Your differences challenge your preconceptions. Once you become receptive to them, they can broaden your perspective.

Differences Teach Us How to Compromise

Since you and your mate have your own unique perspectives, resolving issues will require each of you to listen well and soften your position. The positive outcome is that you both become more adaptable, flexible people. You may even begin to welcome the contribution of your spouse in making decisions.

While raising our children, my husband and I had different ideas about how much money to give them. My husband grew up in a family where finances were limited and he worked hard to ensure he could be generous with his kids. My parents, both teachers, wanted to teach my siblings and me the value of a dollar and expected us to earn our way. Not a few arguments in our marriage centered on my view that Gary was "enabling" our kids and his view that I was "stingy." In time we came to understand that our best decisions were usually made by incorporating both our viewpoints. Unity in diversity brings about interesting and creative resolutions.

Differences Expose Our Selfishness

It is common, especially in early marriage, for spouses to take entrenched positions on a matter, refusing to give in for fear their own needs will not be met. In an intimate relationship, one person's needs often conflict with those of the other partner. The "me" priority is nowhere more exposed than in marriage.

There are countless daily opportunities to choose between what you want or prefer and what your spouse wants or prefers. My husband loves meatloaf and potatoes. I like a salad along with a piece of grilled chicken breast. What shall we have for dinner tonight?

My day off happens to be trash day at our home. My husband's been working all day but the cans need to be brought in off the street. Should I bring them in, since it's typically "his" job? We all have little daily decisions about giving or not giving.

When we're tired or stressed, caring for our mate's needs can be especially inconvenient. We want them to take care of us. Setting ourselves aside to serve our mate is not intuitive. We are inclined to take care of ourselves first. Marriage helps us see the truth about ourselves and calls us to something higher.

Differences Create Mystery

When you first met your spouse, there was likely something intriguing about the ways in which he or she was different from you. You both enjoyed getting to know each other and were pleasantly surprised by some of the attributes you discovered. Not knowing each other completely added an element of mystery to your relationship. It still can.

After we've been married for a while, we think we have our mate all figured out. There is nothing new about them under the sun. We settle in to the faulty notion that there are no more surprises. For some, this feels safe, under control. For others the loss of intrigue feels boring. Either way, there's a problem with this. You've lost your curiosity.

No matter how long you've been married, you cannot know your mate fully. There is always some part of them to discover. Creating a safe space where you can explore your unique dreams, wounds, fantasies, and longings can restore that element of mystery and surprise.

Differences Can Refine Us

Proverbs 27:17 tells us, "As iron sharpens iron, so a friend sharpens a friend" (NLT). In doing life together, you and your spouse rub up against the edges of each other's personality. Over time, differences create friction. That friction, if received as a friend rather than fought as an intruder, can cause you to be more than you were before.

Being receptive is the key. This person you have married can become either a painful thorn in your flesh or a catalyst for your growth, depending on how you choose to respond.

Differences Teach Us to Love

Marriage is designed to transform us by teaching us to love people who are very different from ourselves. Love requires considering the desires, hopes, and longings of your mate. In this way, love stretches us.

Those very ways in which we are different create the potential for the greatest intimacy. You can't be truly intimate with another person if you're invested in conforming them to your image. True intimacy requires an absence of manipulation and an embrace of the differences you each bring to the relationship.

The Bible encourages us to "put on love," to clothe ourselves with love (Col. 3:14). It is not something we already have by birth. It is something we learn. And we learn it in relationship.

Earlier in the passage we are challenged to "bear with each other and forgive one another if any of you has a grievance against someone" (v. 13). "Bearing" with another person means to accept the ways in which they are different, even if that is a burden. Dietrich Bonhoeffer describes "bearing" in this way: "To bear the burden of the other person means involvement with the created reality of the other, to accept and affirm it, and, in bearing with it, to break through to the point where we take joy in it."[8] In bearing with each other, we learn to love the true other—not the one we are trying to fashion for our own benefit and comfort. We take joy in each other's differentness.

> You can't be truly intimate with another person if you're invested in conforming them to your image. True intimacy requires an absence of manipulation and an embrace of the differences you each bring to the relationship.

Like bearing, forgiving is a form of love we learn because we are different from each other. In our different ways of being in the world, we will hurt each other. We extend forgiveness, which releases us from owing each other anything. To free each other in this way is an act of love. Marriage provides lots of opportunity to learn to love through forgiving.

What Embracing Differences Looks Like

How will you know when you have grown in your ability to accept the differences of your mate? You will find yourself curious about their preferences or ways of doing things rather than being annoyed. When your mate expresses an opinion contrary to yours, you will explore their unique vantage point and not be threatened by the disparity with yours. When their priorities or wants are different from yours, you will work with them to find ways of meeting both of your needs—without being disparaging for not aligning with you.

When your spouse reveals their vulnerabilities, you will hold them like a treasure entrusted to you and refuse to use them in any way to hurt your mate. When their protectors are activated, you will see them as attempts to safeguard their tender young parts. You'll be less reactive and less put off, and therefore better able to soothe your partner. In short, you will be openhearted to the nuances and idiosyncrasies of your spouse.

It is not by chance that you have been given your unique mate. Yes, you selected them, but when you married, something happened that's bigger than you and your spouse. You are both being forced to grow in ways you could never have predicted. That growth is primarily due to the differences to which you are learning to adjust.

Whatever your mate most deeply desires will likely be the most difficult thing for you to give. Whatever you most deeply desire will be the hardest for your spouse to give. But in learning to give sacrificially, you will both become more intimate, loving partners.

The differences you experience with your mate provide you with great opportunities. Although some differences are easily accepted and others are painfully difficult, all hold a promise of enriching your lives. If you accept that these are by divine design, you will be more receptive even when they cause inconvenience or discomfort. You can embrace them and learn all that they have to teach you . . . or resist them and miss the opportunity for growth.

If you choose to embrace your mate's differences, you will be stretched. Both of you will grow, but not because you are demanding each other do so. Jesus's call to love our neighbors was not given merely for the sake of our neighbors. Loving people changes us. We are transformed as we embrace the differences of our mate and gracefully learn to love the other as *other.*

Discussion Questions: Chapter 5

Group and Couple Questions

1. Does understanding the God-given physical design of your mate (brain, hormones, anatomy) help you to accept and work with their natural inclinations with more compassion? What do you need to accept about your mate?

2. What are the most significant personality differences between you and your mate? What are the most significant emotional differences? How have you navigated them in the past? What can you do to navigate them more helpfully in the future?

3. Of the six possible purposes for differences in a marriage relationship, which of them have you found to be true for you? Which do you have yet to experience?

4. Read 1 Corinthians 12:14–27. These verses say that just as the physical body is made up of many parts, so the body of Christ is made up of many different parts (all his people are different) and every part has a unique and important purpose. Applying this to marriage, how can we view the differences of our mate? How can we respond to the "weaker" or "unpresentable" parts of our mate? If your and your mate's differences were divinely intended (see v. 18), how might that change your response to their unique needs?

5. Read Colossians 3:13. What does it mean to "bear with" your mate? It is often because your mate is different from you that you have to learn to bear with them at all. It suggests patience and support rather than tolerance and endurance. How do you do so practically?

For Personal Reflection

1. What attracted you to your mate? What did you notice about how your mate was different from you and how did you feel about those differences?

2. Make a list of the ways you and your spouse are different now. Which are easy for you to accept and which cause you marital pain? For those that are difficult, how have you responded to them? Have you diminished or criticized your mate for being different? Have you tried to change them? What do you fear if the difference remains?

3. Does understanding the physical design of your mate (brain, hormones, anatomy) help you to accept and work with their created differences with more compassion? What do you need to accept about your mate?

4. How have your differences benefitted your relationship? How can you be more curious about your differences rather than defensive or critical?

6

Tackle Conflict

All men make mistakes, but married men find out about them sooner.

Red Skelton

When you think of the word *conflict*, what is the first thing that comes to mind? Your last argument with your spouse, the difficult personality of your coworker, the battle of wills you experienced with your parents as a teenager? For most of us, conflict has a negative connotation. Few people have grown up in a home where differences between parents were resolved respectfully and productively. More often conflict was hostile and hurtful or buried deep beneath a subconscious agreement between parents to avoid it at all costs. As a result, we grow up ill-equipped to navigate conflict well. We come to assume that a good relationship will be as conflict-free as possible.

In the survey I conducted in fall 2015, I asked 256 young marrieds what their biggest surprise had been regarding the challenges of married life.[1] The two responses that appeared with the most consistency were surprise at their own selfishness in relationship to their spouse and the difficulty of handling conflict. One responder shared that her most astonishing revelation was to find that "love won't eliminate the possibility of conflict." Many were shocked by how different they were from their spouse and how challenging it was to compromise when each wanted his or her own way. (For more survey results, see appendix E.)

James and Amy were also surprised by the level of conflict in their marriage and made efforts to suppress it. James avoided discussing any issues that might lead to disagreement, and Amy reacted with fear if the volume or pitch became elevated. They consciously desired an honest and open relationship yet were unaware of how their prior experiences of conflict were influencing their responses.

As James described his childhood, it was clear that his parents had very little contention, as they had resigned themselves to low levels of intimacy and engagement. They had chosen to stay together for financial reasons and for the sake of the children but lacked the courage necessary to face their challenges and move through them. Amy's parents suffered a difficult divorce. She had witnessed a great deal of open conflict throughout middle school and a contentious custody battle during high school. James had learned to avoid conflict and withdraw if dissension surfaced. Amy found conflict painful and had no awareness that it could be productive.

James and Amy had both concluded that conflict in marriage was bad. When differences about James's work hours began to surface, Amy suppressed her disappointment but began to increase her texts and phone calls to James during work hours. James became annoyed and assumed Amy should accept the demands of his career but didn't address it with her. One night, when James was especially late, Amy packed a bag and went to her mother's house. As she relayed this incident in counseling, Amy sank back into the sofa, clearly distraught.

"I just don't know what to do," Amy said. "On the one hand, I know James is building his career, but on the other hand I just feel so neglected and hurt. This is not the way I thought our lives would be."

"What do you expect?" James said. "I can't leave before my boss does. If you really wanted me to be successful, you'd be supporting me instead of pulling on me to come home all the time. You can be so unreasonable."

"Is it unreasonable to think you'd want to spend time with your wife? You don't even seem to notice me at all. Even when you're home, you're thinking about work."

"You should be happy I'm thinking about work," James said. "A lot of other people would like my job. I've got to do whatever it takes."

"You weren't like this when we got married. I didn't think you'd become such a workaholic," Amy said.

"Call me whatever you like. You're the selfish one."

James and Amy were no longer able to suppress their conflict. Each of them was unaware of the underlying wounds that were getting triggered in themselves and in the other. Over time, when efforts to minimize conflict failed, James and Amy quickly escalated into name-calling and unproductive fighting that further cemented their view that conflict was always negative and indicated failure. Their experiences of conflict while growing up did not equip them to be able to manage even low levels of disagreement productively. This, combined with their belief that conflict was a sure sign of an unhappy marriage, caused James and Amy to feel defeated.

The Inevitability of Conflict

Confronting the illusion that happy marriages have little to no conflict is necessary in order to embrace the reality of life together. Marital researcher John Gottman challenges this myth with his findings regarding conflict in marriage. After studying more than 650 couples over the course of fourteen years, he found that 69 percent of the problems couples have are perpetual, meaning they will remain problems for the life of the marriage.[2]

The goal for successful couples is not to solve all their problems but to learn to talk about their problems and engage in conflict in ways that don't damage the relationship. The issue is *how* to argue, not *if* you will argue. Happily married couples can have significant differences in personality, interests, habits, and perspectives. They are not surprised by the presence of conflict but learn to negotiate it in a way that remains respectful.

> *The goal for successful couples is not to solve all their problems but to learn to talk about their problems and engage in conflict in ways that don't damage the relationship.*

Psychologist Dan Wile, in his book *After the Honeymoon*, agrees: "When choosing a long-term partner . . . you will inevitably be choosing a particular set of unsolvable problems that you'll be grappling with for the next ten, twenty or fifty years."[3]

Had James and Amy understood that problems and conflict were normal in a healthy marriage, they would have felt less fearful when disagreements occurred. The truth is conflict is not only inevitable but also *essential* to the deepest levels of intimacy you can experience with your mate. Our differences, and the conflict that occurs because of them, are the instruments God uses to confront our selfishness, soften our edges, broaden our perspective, and shape us into the people he desires we become. If we are receptive to changing in response to our areas of conflict, our marriage transforms us into more giving and loving partners.

The Anatomy of a Conflict

Although partners have different styles and tactics of doing conflict, the basic pattern of conflict is fairly easy to deconstruct. One partner says or does something that annoys, hurts, angers, frustrates, or otherwise triggers the other. It can range from a completely innocent comment or action to an honest expression of a concern to something intended to hurt or accuse. In an instant, their partner interprets that behavior or comment through his or her own filters, created by previous experiences and beliefs, and reacts. The more confidence each partner puts in their own interpretation, the less likely they both are to check out their perceptions with their mate. They each see their own views as truth. Each partner reacts to the other's reaction—and the escalation of conflict is off and running.

Consider Sean and Michelle. After dealing with their little one all day, Michelle hopes Sean will do the dishes tonight. But when he comes home, exhausted from a demanding day at work, he heads straight to bed after dinner. Michelle barges into the room and accuses him of selfishness for not helping with the dishes. Sean asks Michelle why she didn't ask him to do the dishes. She retorts that she shouldn't have to—if he really loved her, he would know what she needed. Sean reminds Michelle of the stressful season he's in at work. Michelle dismisses this as an excuse. Their competing needs, coupled with misinterpretation, accusation, and defensiveness, cause their conflict to escalate, leaving both feeling discouraged and disconnected.

Our Brains in Conflict

The human brain is hardwired to protect us when we are in any potential danger. It is equipped with a fear response that urges us to fight, flee, or freeze. During stress or periods of instability, the emotional center of our brain (the amygdala) is activated and takes offline the part of our brain that reasons and cooperates (the prefrontal cortex). This emotional system of the brain is directed toward self-protection and self-preservation. When we feel threatened, a flood of chemicals from the amygdala locks us into our heightened emotional state and makes it difficult for us to work through a conflict.

As children, when we felt threatened by the withdrawal, disapproval, or anger of a parent, we developed protectors to cope with our fear of rejection, harm, or loss. And so some of us avoid or analyze, others get angry or judge, and still others seek to please or detach. We carry our particular set of protectors into our marriage relationship. When our mate triggers our fear responses, our protectors jump in to ensure our safety. Marital conflict is, in essence, a battle between these protectors, fueled by our respective amygdalas. With our emotional systems thus activated, we are unable to listen, empathize, or resolve.

One young wife expressed it well: "I was surprised by how vicious our fights can be. We have always been expressive, but marriage has taken it to a whole new level."

When we are calm, a more social system in the brain is accessible. That part of the brain seeks closeness, emotional bonding, and attachment. This social system interacts with the prefrontal cortex, the part of the brain that allows us to process information, resolve problems, and deal with complex social stimuli.

To the extent that we are able to calm our brains, we become more able to process conflict productively and to connect with our mate.

Additionally, the prefrontal cortex sends signals to the parts of the brain that release oxytocin, the hormone most responsible for our caring and bonding behaviors. To the extent that we are able to calm our brains, we become more able to process conflict productively and to connect with our mate.

It is nearly impossible to resolve problems or be empathic when you get triggered by your mate and are "hijacked" by your emotional brain. In order for each of you to understand the other's feelings and positions, there has to be enough safety to allow your reactive protectors to relax. Once they are calmed, vulnerability and receptivity are possible.

Understanding your mate's wounds and hurts of childhood, which led to the development of their protectors, can enable you to be less reactive to their protectors and more empathetic toward their young wounded parts. That empathy will calm you both and allow for the bonding social system to emerge rather than the fear/protective system.

Calming the System

Creating enough calm and safety to navigate the conflict you and your spouse will inevitably face is imperative for marital success. Calming your system involves paying attention to your triggers, your tactics (what you do when you get triggered), and your protectors so they don't derail the conversation. It requires learning how to approach your mate in a soft way that assures them of your love, regardless of the problem you want to address.

Creating an environment that promotes productive conflict involves sensitivity to timing. Approaching issues when you are both rested and undistracted enough to be emotionally available is crucial. Hold off on important conversations when one or both of you are stressed and have little margin to have a meaningful discussion. If you are in an extended season of stress, with no foreseeable relief in sight, set a time for the conversation that allows you both to prepare mentally and emotionally. This will increase the chance of a good outcome.

Take note of what causes you to become reactive to your mate. What triggers you? Is it when your mate's voice has a certain tone to it? When they use certain words? When they shut down? Do you have a reaction when your mate gets highly emotional or when you feel put down, blamed, or criticized? Do you tend to react when they have a different opinion than you do or when they misunderstand what you're saying? What feelings come up for you when your mate does those things?

Also pay attention to what you do when you react—your tactics. When you feel unsafe, do you throw gas on the fire? Do you get critical, blame your spouse, or become defensive? Do you resort to name-calling, threaten divorce, or belittle your spouse's family? Do you use manipulation or punishment to get your spouse to behave differently or see things your way? Do you become stoically logical or overly emotional? Do you joke or use sarcasm to avoid honest engagement? Do you disconnect or shut down? Chances are you've been using your tactics for some time, which may make them difficult to detect.

Seth and Amber were unaware of how their tactics were setting off a cycle of reactivity, which precluded healthy conversations. Seth minimized the impact of his anger on Amber and became increasingly incensed when she, in her anxiety and hurt, disconnected from him. Amber's retreat and sexual avoidance felt like criticism and withholding to Seth. He responded by demeaning Amber, which only led her to pull away more.

Nick and Jennifer had no idea they were triggering old wounds in each other. Nick's dad had abandoned the family when he was four. As the oldest son, he had become his mother's confidant and helper. Jennifer had a critical dad and was hoping to find in her husband the approval and attention she lacked. When Nick catered to his mom's needs and frequent phone calls, Jennifer felt the sting of his divided interest. She reacted by attacking Nick and demanding he cut off his relationship with his mother.

In fear of disappointing his mother or his wife, Nick tried to please his wife while maintaining a covert relationship with his mother. Nick and Jennifer needed to become aware that they were reenacting their childhood roles and see how their reactions were re-wounding each other.

Gottman's marital research concluded that because 69 percent of couples' problems are perpetual, the goal is not to solve them as much as it is to have conversations about them without doing harm or causing further hurt. In order to have such conversations it is essential to be able to notice your triggers and tactics in an argument, as they give you needed information about your protectors that are at work. Once you are able to identify your protectors, you can appreciate their efforts to make you safe and ask them to step back and trust you to have the needed conversation with your spouse. Using the "Identify Your Protectors" exercise in chapter 4 will help bring clarity to what is going on inside you and allow you to speak *for* your parts instead of *from* them.[4]

Becoming aware of your triggers and tactics and your own protectors that get activated will help you to slow the reactive process and bring more calm to your discussions. Additionally, learning how to approach a difficult subject with your spouse will go a long way toward ensuring those conversations will be helpful to your relationship.

Engaging Your Partner

Whether you or your mate brings up the issue, how useful a conversation will be to the health of your marriage can be determined within the first five seconds of engagement. If you approach the conversation with an angry, impatient, demanding, or frustrated tone, it's likely the discussion will go downhill from there. If you approach it with a soft, calm, appreciative tone, the possibility of having a productive marital conversation is significantly improved.

As you begin a sensitive conversation, the following guidelines can help you engage your mate appropriately:

1. *Check for protectors.* If you feel anger, anxiety, or any other feeling that may hinder a positive outcome, take a few minutes to check in with yourself, notice how you're feeling, and ask any protectors that seem "on guard" to step back and relax.

2. *Clarify your intentions.* When you decide to address an area of conflict with your mate, ask yourself what your goal or hope is in bringing up the issue. Do you want to persuade your mate to agree with you or are you seeking mutual understanding? Do you want to win an argument or foster closeness? Do you want to get your mate to change or are you

willing to compromise? Consider the needs of your mate and of your marriage.

3. *Approach gently.* Starting a conversation with a harsh tone or "edge" will likely trigger some defenses in your mate and reduce the likelihood you will have a useful conversation. The Bible says it well: "A gentle answer turns away wrath, but a harsh word stirs up anger" (Prov. 15:1). Softening your tone as you approach your mate will do wonders in promoting a positive outcome. Offering an affirmation or expressing appreciation for some aspect of your mate or their behavior can help them lower their defenses as they are reassured you see the good in them.

4. *State your hope.* When you ask your mate to discuss the problem with you, let them know the positive outcome you're hoping for (increased understanding, compromise, a resolution that will benefit both). For example, "Seth, I'd like to talk with you about our upcoming visit to your parents. I want it to go smoothly, so I'd like to discuss some concerns I have."

Speaking More Than Your Mind

Once you have set the stage for the conversation by approaching your mate gently, you will want to express your issue in a way that is non-blaming and increases the chances you will be heard by your mate. To do so, it is helpful to use an "I" statement.[5] An "I" statement allows you to assert yourself, sharing your thoughts, feelings, and hopes without putting your mate on the defensive.

The "I" statement is constructed of three parts: what happened, the feeling you had when it happened, and why you suspect that feeling came up for you. For example, "When we visited your parents last time, and your mom criticized our parenting and you did not respond, I felt frustrated and resentful because I was hoping you would set a boundary with her." This statement is direct, honest, and clearly expresses the issue and feelings without blaming.

This approach is far better than an attacking, blaming "you" statement such as, "You don't stand up for me when your mom is critical," or "You care about your mom's feelings more than mine!" Such statements will provoke defensiveness in your mate and reduce the chances they will respond well.

When you express your feelings in an "I" statement, it is important to use a one-word feeling (see the "Feeling Words" list in appendix A) that expresses your internal experience, such as, "I felt resentful," or "I felt lonely." If you find yourself saying "I felt *that* . . ." or "I felt *like* . . ." you are probably not expressing a feeling but rather a thought. It is important to express your feelings, as this gives your partner an opportunity for deeper understanding and empathy.

The Art of Listening

Listening to another person for any length of time is not easy. If we are honest, most of us will admit that we'd rather be listened to and understood than to listen to our mate. I want my husband to be riveted to my concerns about my day, but when he wants to offload the stresses of his, my attention seems to wander. Why is listening so hard?

First, we are distracted. Life is full and our minds are busy. Men's brains tend to compartmentalize. When they are focused on one thing, they have difficulty shifting to a space where they are attentive and available verbally. As multitaskers, women are used to having their attention in many places at once. They too have difficulty narrowing their focus to be fully attentive to their husbands' concerns.

Second, we are selfish. Most of us are more invested in having our mate agree with us or hear us out than in listening carefully to them. We value being understood more than understanding our mate. We don't want to hear anything that goes against (or that we think goes against) our positions. Also, when we are angry with our mate, we may selfishly refuse to listen to their positions as a form of protest or punishment.

Third, we have our own filters. We are oblivious to the fact that the messages our mate is sending and what we're hearing can be very different. That's because we filter what our mate says based on our own experiences, beliefs, and perspectives. We fail to listen well because we attach meaning to what our mate is saying based on our own filters and we react to them as if our interpretation is accurate. As a result, our mate feels unheard.

Finally, listening is hard work. It takes setting ourselves aside for the time being and really focusing on the feelings, thoughts, and concerns of our mate. It requires effort and intentionality. Though difficult, listening—more than anything else—communicates respect, caring, and love: respect for your mate's unique experience, care for them above yourself in that moment, and love that says, "You are important to me, and I want to take the time to hear you."

So how do we listen well to our mate in a way that communicates love and facilitates understanding? Here is a checklist you might find helpful:

1. *Prepare yourself to listen.* You may have some apprehension about having a discussion on a particular area of conflict. Check for any anxiety, anger, or resentment that may interfere with your ability to be curious about your mate. These emotions serve to protect and defend you. If you detect any of these protectors, invite them to step back. Ask yourself if you are able to be openhearted as you listen.

2. *Invite your mate to share their thoughts and feelings with you.* Be receptive and show them you're available by your eye contact, body language, and demeanor. If at any point you find yourself reacting inside to what your mate is saying, let your mate know and take a moment to calm that part of you and see if it's willing to step back and allow you to listen.

3. *Check out your assumptions.* We all have filters through which we listen to others. These filters cause us to assume and attach certain meanings to what other people are saying. Before you jump to a conclusion, ask your mate to explain their intended meaning. Don't assume you can read their mind. Have the humility to recognize that you have filters.

4. *Demonstrate respect by allowing your mate to speak from their perspective.* Allow for differentness. Coach yourself to listen with the sole intention of understanding your partner's world. If they say something about you that hurts your feelings, remember it is not necessarily the truth about you but rather their perspective.

5. *Respond to your mate's sharing by periodically reflecting back to them what you heard them say.* This will allow you to clarify what you've heard. It also assures your mate that you are hearing them clearly. Don't interpret or put your spin on what they said. Ask if you got it right. If not, be open to receiving clarification.

6. *Be present.* If you're too tired or preoccupied when your mate wants to talk, set a time soon thereafter when they may have your undivided attention. Remove any distractions—turn off the television, computer, and cell phones. If you have children, choose a time when you will most likely not be interrupted.

7. At the conclusion of your mate's sharing, *let them know what makes sense to you about what they've said and offer empathy for their feelings.* Remember, this does not mean they are completely right and you are wrong, only that you can understand their experience and perspective. You might also ask what they might need from you to feel soothed.

Listening attentively to your mate is a gift you give that reaps great rewards for both of you. It tells your spouse that they are important to you and that you value their thoughts and feelings. Listening is like the oil that keeps your car running smoothly. Without it, and the steady lubrication it provides, the engine will sputter and die.

Repair in Conflict

The ability to repair in the midst of a conflict is not easy but it is essential to keep both of your emotional systems calmed and available for understanding and resolution. Once an argument escalates, a husband's blood pressure and heart rate will elevate more quickly and remain elevated longer than his wife's. Men become emotionally flooded more easily than women and take longer to soothe internally.[6]

Listening is like the oil that keeps your car running smoothly. Without it, and the steady lubrication it provides, the engine will sputter and die.

A wife's criticism can send her husband into this flooded state. In response, he reacts with "fight or flight." Husbands who are trying not to fight will often withdraw or stonewall to cope with their flooded state and avoid further escalation. Wives tend to interpret this withdrawal as avoidance or rejection and react with further criticism or negativity.

To stop this reactive cycle, both husband and wife can make efforts toward repairing the conversation. Gottman's research revealed that men who enjoyed happy, stable marriages were taking the lead in de-escalating the negativity in conflicts. When their wives became angry, disappointed, or hurt, these husbands would not respond in kind. Instead, they would remain neutral for at least five seconds, which allowed their heart rate to drop so they could respond more positively. Wives who are aware of the impact of their criticism and negativity can learn to share their feelings and disappointments in a noncritical way using "I" statements.

Both partners can take initiative to repair an escalating argument. If you observe either you or your mate getting triggered, slow things down by suggesting a brief time-out, with a commitment to return to the discussion at a specified time. Studies show that it can take more than twenty minutes, particularly for men, to soothe physiologically after being activated, so this may be a good length for a time-out. A simple "I'm sorry" for a poorly chosen word or gesture can go a long way to keep the conversation on track. Restating your positive goal for the dialogue or asking for a "do over" can also serve as a restart button for the discussion.

If you find yourself slipping into a critical, contemptuous, or superior mindset, you are likely to use tactics that will hurt your relationship. Stop yourself, let your mate know you've noticed that one or more of your protectors has jumped in, and take a few moments to regroup. Often, you are not aware of your own parts kicking in, but if you notice your mate becoming defensive, that could be their reaction to the tactics of your protectors. Ask your mate what in your tone or words triggered their response. This will allow them to observe themselves and diffuse while allowing you to course-correct, which ultimately makes for a more productive conversation.

These efforts at repair can help you stay connected and talk through your issues to create deeper levels of understanding. Awareness of your protectors, and their tactics of defensiveness and attack, can help you take responsibility for how you react in conflict and intercept their intervention. Avoiding criticism and withdrawal will help your mate feel more available for understanding and connection.

Hot Topics

In the course of every marriage, issues surface that trigger a strong emotional reaction. Some topics are so hot they are hard to even discuss. If an issue is loaded with negative energy, it likely has deep roots in childhood and touches a core need for respect, security, or love. When couples get into heated battles, they often get stuck discussing the content of the issue from their entrenched positions but rarely get to the deeper longings and fears that fuel the intense energy surrounding the topic.

Most of the hot issues you will experience as a couple are perpetual, meaning they will likely be there for the life of your relationship.[7] Sound like bad news? Not really. If you continue to think that these issues are solvable, you will likely be stuck in patterns that try to convince your mate to see things as you do, and vice versa. You will continue to use the common tactics of criticism, put-downs, manipulation, sarcasm, and so on to win the argument. Accepting that the issue will likely be there for the life of your marriage can help you release your expectation that it will be resolved by using your solution. Then you can loosen your grip on efforts to force the compliance or agreement of your spouse.

Instead, you can take responsibility for declawing the topic and developing a way of talking about the issue that respects your different vantage points. You can begin to hear each other with less of an agenda and form compromises that honor both positions. "A compromise that works, even though not ideal, is better than a brilliant solution imposed upon a resentful partner."[8] Together you can find a middle ground that allows for more of a win-win outcome. When the issue surfaces again, you will have a better feeling about it and can engage in the conversation with positive anticipation that you are able to discuss it in a healthy way.

Using the steps discussed in this chapter—to calm yourself, engage your partner, share your thoughts and feelings, and listen well to your mate—will help you turn painful conflict into conflict that increases understanding and intimacy. These steps can be applied to any conflict you have, including the hot topics of life balance, finances, in-laws, and sex.

Life Balance

Balancing time with your spouse, career, friends, children, and hobbies can be a challenge. One young mother responded to the survey, "Our biggest challenge has been a super busy schedule. I think we are subconsciously trying to hold on to parts of our single life when it comes to friendships." If you have experienced an extensive and active social life before marriage, learning to reserve time to invest in your marriage and family life can be tough. The truth is you only have so many hours in a day and so many relationships to which you can meaningfully devote yourself.

Balancing career and family can also be difficult. Children usually come along just as one or both of you are striving to establish yourselves in your careers. If you divide to conquer—one of you being the breadwinner while the other stays home with children—the need to have frequent communication is especially important, as your energies and priorities may diverge. If you both choose to work outside the home, the challenge of schedules, planning, child care, and the like can take their toll on your relationship. The key in both scenarios is to keep in regular communication, learn to compromise, and do your best to attend to the needs of your mate.

Many couples fail to discuss life balance or make intentional choices about their time. They allow the demands of careers or children to become their primary focus. These couples are the ones who wake up one day to say, "We've just grown apart," or "All we have left in common are the kids." If you prioritize work or children over your spouse's needs, your relationship will suffer. Working through these conflicts early can set your marriage on course to stay connected through all the years ahead.

If this is a hot topic for you, you might consider doing the life balance exercise at the end of the chapter.

Finances

Managing finances can be a major source of friction for couples. One young mom was surprised to realize how their "different financial habits can drastically affect marriage." Another husband mentioned that "money is at the root of our serious fights."

You and your spouse came into marriage with different ways of thinking about money and different habits for saving and spending. It is also likely that you each attach a different meaning to money. For some, money is deeply tied to security. Scarcity of it brings fear—fear of being an inadequate provider, fear of going without, fear of going under.

For others, money symbolizes freedom—freedom to purchase and enjoy material possessions. For these people, placing limits on spending feels constraining.

Habits about money are developed during childhood. Most couples will need to learn to communicate their deeper needs and fears in order to come to a willingness to compromise and work together to build their financial future.

The issue of finances is almost never about money. It is usually about fear, control, power, helplessness, feeling unappreciated, and so forth. If you can get at the root feelings, the issue can be declawed.

Take time to share with each other how your respective families dealt with money and what it has come to represent to you. What emotions come up as you think about money? If this is a hot topic for you, try working through the finance exercise at the end of the chapter.

In-Laws

When you marry, you inherit a family—for better or for worse. Your spouse's relatives will undoubtedly be quite different from yours. Unless there have been serious issues with your own family, you will likely favor them above your mate's, as they are familiar and seem to do things the "right" way.

Sometimes parents can be intrusive and attempt to control their adult children's decisions. In other cases they are distant, even if their children desire for them to be more connected and involved. Defining yourselves as a couple and finding a good balance between including parents appropriately in your lives and setting necessary limits to any interference is an important effort. But relating to your in-laws with love and limits can be a challenging task.

Sometimes the problems with in-laws have to do with leaving and cleaving. You and/or your spouse may have difficulty separating from your family of origin. The emotional or physical needs of a parent or your own need to receive the approval and affirmation of your parents can keep you tied to them.

The Bible wisely talks about the importance of leaving your parents in order to attach well to your spouse. "A man leaves his father and mother and is united to his wife, and they become one flesh" (Gen. 2:24). "Leaving" involves not only a physical move but also emotional detachment. In order to unite fully with your spouse, it is important to leave the security provided by your parents and risk the transference of loyalty and priority to your spouse. It is a risk because you don't know your mate as well as you know your parents, and your spouse doesn't know you as well as your parents do. But release is necessary if you are to experience the bonding and uniting necessary for a successful, healthy, happy marriage.

It is not uncommon for one or both spouses to experience difficulty separating from a parent. In my work with young couples, when the husband has been the emotional support for his mother, perhaps due to his parents' divorce or his mother's feeling of disconnection from her spouse, he can have a more difficult time leaving his mother and cleaving to his wife. This issue must be acknowledged and addressed in order to set appropriate limits on Mom's neediness and the role of son-turned-husband.

In order to unite fully with your spouse, it is important to leave the security provided by your parents and risk the transference of loyalty and priority to your spouse.

I have also seen daughters who remain attached to their mothers as a form of security. Often these daughters-turned-wives are unaware that their closeness with Mom interferes with the bond they need to create with their husband. Transferring loyalty and setting appropriate boundaries will be necessary for a healthy marriage.

Some adult children fear having discussions with their parents about family boundaries. They're afraid of hurting their feelings as well as the distance that may be created. You cannot control the hurt your parents may feel, but if boundaries are discussed lovingly and firmly, they will likely adjust eventually.

This courageous step will protect your marriage from harm and will help you bond as a couple. When your spouse knows you are willing to make them your top priority, their relationship with your parents will likely improve.

If this is an area of concern for you, check out the in-laws exercise at the end of this chapter.

Sex

You and your mate have differing sexual needs. Because men typically have a higher sex drive than women, they typically want to engage in sex more often. Their ability to compartmentalize allows most men to switch gears from work or another activity to sex in an instant. Women, on the other hand, being multitaskers, have more difficulty reining in the demands of their day to be present for the enjoyment of physical intimacy. They tend to add it to their to-do list and get frustrated with their husband's more frequent interest.

Sex is a common perpetual issue that has, at its core, deep needs that must be recognized.

Women long to feel loved. For most women, sexual intimacy is about connection with their husband. They typically feel more available for sex when they feel their husband's devotion and caring.

142

When a husband becomes absorbed in work or other priorities, a wife tends to focus elsewhere—on children, friends, her own work. When he is ready for sex, she has difficulty turning on a dime. As conflict escalates over this issue, she views his steady interest as "all about him" and his gratification, not about her need for tender care and connection.

Men's heightened need for sexual connection is built in. For men, sex has a lot to do with feeling adequate and alive. When a husband feels rejected by his wife, or fails to give her pleasure, he feels deficient. When he is dismissed or put off for extended periods, he feels a loss of vitality. These feelings can be hidden beneath a veneer of anger, criticism, or withdrawal.

Husbands: tending to your wife's longing to feel loved and cared for can go a long way in making for mutually enjoyable lovemaking.

Wives: inviting your husband to talk about his feelings and working together to find ways to meet both of your needs is important.

For more specifics about the issue of sexual intimacy, details on how to navigate the differences, and exercises to help you and your mate experience a mutually satisfying sex life, read chapter 9.

The Creativity of Conflict

Having the tough conversations necessary to manage conflict well is a fundamental step toward a healthy marriage. Avoiding the issues has never brought a couple to rich levels of intimacy. Does that mean every area of difference needs to be addressed? Not necessarily. There are some situations that are not big enough to require working through formally. They can be overlooked as a way of offering grace.

Some conflict can be averted by learning to repair the conversation when it first begins to get off track. Other issues will require a more intentional time to sit down and work things through. By taking the steps offered in this chapter, you will be able to successfully navigate even the most challenging issues in your marriage.

Conflict is never easy. It brings us face-to-face with the worst in ourselves and the worst in our mate. But what if one of God's purposes in marriage, perhaps the primary purpose, is to shape us into the person he wants us to become through the inevitable conflicts of married life?

When I began to accept the very real possibility that my conflicts with my husband might have a divine purpose, I began to see our arguments in a different light. If "iron sharpens iron" (Prov. 27:17), maybe the friction we experienced could bear fruit in a way I'd never imagined. Growth is painful. As Tim Keller points out, "The merged life of marriage brings you into the closest, most inescapable contact with another person possible. And that means not only that you see each other close-up, but that you are forced to deal with the flaws and sins of one another."[9]

Remember, if you are in the trenches of difficult conflict, God is doing a work in you and in your spouse in ways that you may only see very dimly, if at all, in the present moment. In Isaiah 55:8 God says, "My thoughts are not your thoughts, neither are your ways my ways." His ways are different from ours. The path he has prepared for you may not resemble the one in your dreams. But his path is far better and even more beautiful than you can imagine.

God is using your marriage to shape you and your mate into the people he created you to be. What other relationship in life has the ability to expose and challenge our self-interest, our hurtful habits, and our defensive responses like marriage? Only marriage and the conflict we experience through the intimate sharing of life has the power to do this, because there is no other relationship that so exposes our wounds and challenges us to love unselfishly.

Conflict is, in essence, the most creative component of your married life. Through it, God is making you and your marriage into something altogether new.

Discussion Questions: Chapter 6

Group and Couple Questions

1. When you hear the word *conflict*, what comes to mind? Share how conflict was handled in your home growing up.

2. Describe how you feel when your mate brings up an issue in a soft tone versus in a harsh way. Read Proverbs 15:1. Why is it important to approach a sensitive conversation with your spouse in a gentle way?

3. Read Proverbs 18:13 and James 1:19–20. What do these verses say about the importance of listening?

4. Can you identify your protectors that get triggered in conflict? Can you begin to identify the patterns you and your spouse get caught in when in conflict? Read Proverbs 12:18, James 1:26, and 1 Peter 3:9–11. Why is it important to calm protectors before or during a conflict?

5. Read Proverbs 15:18 and 16:18. How do pride and anger impact the escalation of conflict?

6. Which of the "hot topics" create difficulty for you as a couple? Share what you intend to do differently based on your reading of this chapter.

7. Make a commitment to the group to do one of the couple exercises below and check in with each other at your next meeting to see how it went.

For Personal Reflection

1. How was conflict handled in your home growing up? Is the way you handle conflict with your spouse similar or dissimilar?

2. Notice your personal protectors that get activated in arguments with your spouse. Using the "Identify Your

Protectors" exercise in chapter 4, review your most recent argument and see if you can notice your feelings, thoughts, and reactions.

3. What makes it difficult for you to diffuse or repair an active argument? What can your spouse do to help you calm yourself? Let them know.

Couple Exercises

1. Speaker-Listener Exercise
Select an issue that has been a source of mild conflict. Agree to listen to each other for ten minutes on your perspectives of the issue. Decide who will be the speaker first and who will be the listener. If you are the speaker, review the sections on "Engaging Your Partner" and "Speaking More Than Your Mind." If you are the listener, review the listening checklist from the section "The Art of Listening." Be sure to end the conversation with item 7.

2. Life Balance Exercise
For this exercise to be successful, each of you needs to allow your mate to express their true feelings without judgment.

a. Make a pie chart of the way you currently spend your time. How much time do you allot to work, spouse, kids, friends, hobbies, extended family, other? Compare your chart with your spouse's chart. Discuss how they are similar and different.

b. Next, make a pie chart of the way you ideally want to spend your time. Share with your mate.

c. Taking into consideration both of your needs, each of you make a third pie chart that reflects a realistic compromise agreeable to you both. Think of two things each of you could do, within the next two weeks, to move from the first chart to the third.

146

3. Finance Exercise

    a. Check to see if you have any protectors that might need attention before you begin this discussion. Then ask yourself the following:

        1) How was money handled in my home growing up? How did this affect my thinking and habits?

        2) What is my deepest fear where money is concerned?

        3) What is most important to me when making financial decisions?

    b. Share these answers with your mate.

    c. Brainstorm family goals regarding money management. Taking into consideration the deepest needs of you and your spouse, determine three goals you have for the coming six months related to saving, spending, and becoming financial partners. For instance, save $500 per month for one year, trim eating-out expenses, start a savings account for our child, and so forth. You may want to consider a simple budgeting plan that looks at current monthly income, expenses, and desired savings in order to determine your goals.

4. In-Laws Exercise

    a. Take an honest inventory. Is there any way you have prioritized your parents or family of origin over your spouse? If so, offer your spouse a sincere apology.

    b. If one of you has had difficulty with leaving your parents emotionally and uniting to your spouse, acknowledge it. What feelings come up when you think about becoming less dependent/connected with your parents and more with your spouse? What needs are getting met by staying connected with your parents? How can your spouse begin to meet some of these core needs? Share these needs with your spouse.

    c. Invite your spouse to have a conversation regarding how each of you would ideally like to relate to each of your parents.

1) How much time would you like to spend with each side of the family?

2) When visiting your spouse's family, is there any way in which you would like your mate to stand by you?

3) Are there any boundaries you would like or need to set to ensure your parents understand that you are a separate, independent family and your spouse is your priority? When setting limits with intrusive parents, it is important for the one whose parents are overstepping their roles to be the one to set boundaries. This can be done lovingly by stating, "Mom, Dad—we love you and want to have a good relationship with you. We also feel it is important for us as a couple/family to (determine where to spend the holidays, make our own decisions, start our own traditions, and so forth). We look forward to spending time with you and would appreciate it if you would accept our desires." If there is an expectation of daily or frequent phone calls or visits, it may be necessary to advise your parent that you intend to contact them regularly but less frequently.

d. If you are not financially independent, make a plan to become so and relate your intentions to your contributing parent(s). (When parents are financially supporting their adult child, they tend to conclude that they have a say in the child's decisions, which does not bode well for married life.)

7

Let Go

Begin challenging your own assumptions. Your assumptions are
your windows on the world. Scrub them off every once in a while,
or the light won't come in.

Alan Alda

Our deep longings for intimate relationship are there by design. We
are made to enjoy meaningful connection and a shared life. In an
effort to ensure our longings get met, we often cling to strategies
that we believe will help satisfy them. Many of these strategies,
however, actually hinder the very thing we are trying to achieve.
Identifying these, and letting them go, is necessary to enjoy the
friendship and fullness of married life. But we rarely stop to evaluate how our beliefs came about or how effective our strategies
actually are.

Pride can get in the way of an honest exploration. We like to
think we perceive ourselves correctly. However, if we dig deep
enough to locate the real reason behind the beliefs we hold that
are harmful to our marriage, we often find fear.

Fear is the primary reason we cling to our detrimental beliefs—fear of being alone, fear of rejection, fear of a loss of security, fear of failure, fear of not being enough, fear of not having everything we want in life. These fears, if left unacknowledged, can wreak havoc on a marriage.

If you have a core fear of being alone or rejected, you may become anxious or angry when your mate fails to meet your expectations. You might believe they should be able to read your mind if they really loved you. When they fail to come through for you, you protect your heart by casting your mate in a very negative light, seeing their every effort as poorly executed and insufficient.

If your core fear is not being enough for your mate, you may believe you need to do everything in your power just to be adequate. You place demands on your spouse, believing if they are met that will confirm your value to them. You shut down your mate's expression of their own needs to avoid feeling incompetent. You resent what seems like criticism and pull away from your mate to distance yourself from their needs and desires.

Most fears are the product of unmet needs in childhood. Identifying the original source of your fear is key to letting go of those things that are hindering your marriage.

Let Go of Perfectionism

While growing up with a critical and disapproving dad, Jennifer learned she had to do things perfectly to avoid his stern rebukes. She didn't allow herself a margin of error, whether doing chores or homework. When she would miss the mark of perfection, she berated herself and pushed herself harder. She never questioned her dad's exacting expectations or her own standards. Perfection ensured her dad would stay connected to her, and anything short of perfection would threaten that connection.

Jennifer measured her self-worth by her flawless performance. To outsiders, she looked like a model mother and wife. Inside she was tormented by her pursuit of the ever-elusive, unattainable ideal and the profound feeling of insecurity she felt at the thought of missing her mark.

When she would succeed at accomplishing a goal, the sweetness of the attainment would not last long, as her self-critical protector would jump in and ensure she kept up her exhaustive efforts.

Jennifer's insecure attachment to her father and the perfectionism that protected her from rejection created demands on her young marriage. She expected Nick to do things perfectly and she became highly critical when he did not meet her standards. When Nick failed to perform chores that she knew needed to be done, Jennifer accused him of intentionally ignoring what she wanted.

She clung tightly to her belief that Nick's failure to come through for her meant he didn't love her enough. Having suffered the withdrawal of her father's approval when she didn't perform, Jennifer came to equate perfection with connection. Anything short of her high standard was a threat to her marriage and, therefore, intolerable.

As we began in therapy, Jennifer didn't realize her expectations were unrealistic. She was also unaware of the fear that fueled her demands. Jennifer's deep fear of loss of connection and disapproval underlay her compulsive need to have everything just right. Her core mistaken belief that she would be unacceptable if she didn't do things perfectly and her desperate desire to avoid criticism, deprived her of joy and served as a heavy weight in her marriage. In time, Jennifer was able to see how her expectations derived from her fear, why she clung to them, and the havoc they were wreaking on her marriage. She was able to calm her exacting protectors and offer compassion to her young, wounded part that was driving her behavior.

Let Go of Mind Reading

I recently read a blog post titled "24 Signs You've Found Your Soul Mate."[1] It got 52,030 "likes" in six days. Among the "signs" offered were these: "You can convey what you're thinking by just looking at each other," and "They know exactly what to do to calm you down when you're mad, to help relieve your stress, or to cheer you up."

The notion of finding that one person who knows you so thoroughly you never have to express yourself is alluring. It absolves you of communicating your needs effectively. But this assumption has caused much unnecessary resentment and marital pain.

Just as we hope our spouse is so in tune with us that they can anticipate our needs, we pride ourselves on being able to read our mate's mind. We make assumptions that seem perfectly reasonable to us.

Just as we hope our spouse is so in tune with us that they can anticipate our needs, we pride ourselves on being able to read our mate's mind.

Your wife is preoccupied with your child's homework? She must not care to hear about your day. Your husband unknowingly tracks mud into the house? He doesn't care about your time or effort spent cleaning. Your wife points out an available parking space? Of course she thinks you're an idiot. Your husband fails to buy you what you hinted at for your birthday? He doesn't care about what you really want. We make assumptions based on our own filters, our conditioned beliefs about what certain behaviors mean.

We are so confident in our assumptions of what our mate's motives are, we refuse to believe any explanation on their part. Instead we look for evidence to support what we believe to be true. And inevitably we will find it. The problem is, we exclude from our awareness any evidence that would dispute our assumption.

We attempt to mind-read in order to protect ourselves from feeling devalued or unloved. If we can anticipate what's in our mate's head, we will be able to defend against it. This protects us from being vulnerable and risking hurt. The truth is we can't really know what is in anyone else's mind. Assuming that we can leaves our mate feeling misunderstood and hopeless. Letting go of the tendency to jump to conclusions is imperative to having clear communication and a better relationship.

Next time you catch yourself assuming the worst about your spouse, check out your assumptions. Rather than concluding, *They don't care about me or the kids*, ask your spouse what they meant by what they said or did. Give them the chance to clarify. Acknowledging that your spouse may think differently than you do about certain things demonstrates respect. If you're going to assume anything, assume positively.

Let Go of Negative Interpretations

Michelle sends Sean several texts throughout the workday, and he doesn't respond. She assumes he is upset with her or intentionally ignoring her. But the truth is he had a series of back-to-back meetings and didn't check his phone. When he gets home, Michelle lets him have it. Tired from such a long day, Sean lashes back.

When our mate says or does things that hurt or disappoint us, our internal reaction is usually to protect ourselves. We view our mate's actions in the worst possible light so we won't become vulnerable. Our protectors push us to conclude, and act, quickly.

When we negatively interpret our mate's actions, and act accordingly, we trigger their protectors and they launch their own defense system.

When we negatively interpret our mate's actions, and act accordingly, we trigger their protectors and they launch their own defense system. Once this escalation occurs, communication derails. If we consistently interpret our mate's thoughts and motives as negative, we can cause them to feel hopeless and unheard.

How can you get out of your tendency to negatively interpret your spouse's behavior? Here are a few suggestions.

When you realize you're beginning to go down a negative mental path, tell yourself to slow down. Ask, *Is there any possibility that I'm seeing this incorrectly?* This takes humility. We all like to think we're right. But if you consider the probability that you haven't interpreted everything accurately, you can then ask your mate to help you understand what happened and be open to their response.

If you're confident you're right, it will be tempting to dismiss their response as an excuse. Dismissing your mate's clarification says more about your need to be right than a desire to truly understand.

Try giving your spouse the benefit of the doubt. Looking for evidence that supports their explanation will help you gain a more positive frame of mind.

Let Go of Unreasonable Expectations

Our expectations come out of previous experiences or information gathered from outside sources. Do you believe your spouse should behave in a certain way because of something you read or viewed in the media? The notion of a continuously scintillating sexual connection between loving couples may be the stuff of magazines, billboards, and steamy romance novels, but it is not reality. Having a continuously strong emotional connection with your mate, free from the interruptions and distractions of work, kids, and other commitments, is not realistic. Connection ebbs and flows in every good marriage.

If you believe your expectations are reasonable and justified, ask yourself where those expectations came from. Is it possible there's some kind of fear involved?

Exploring the fears underlying your expectations can help you shift the focus from your mate to your own protectors. It will increase your self-awareness and help you develop more reasonable expectations.

Let Go of Comparisons

It's tempting to compare your mate with other people's spouses. You notice a friend's husband giving his wife a hug or dropping his preschooler off at school and you think, *I bet they have a great marriage. I wish I had somebody like that!* Because we have a front-row seat to our mate's flaws, moods, and weaknesses, we imagine that life with another spouse must be significantly better.

Underlying most comparison is a fear that we won't get what we need. Out of this fear, we try to manage every detail of our lives so we can be assured of our own fulfillment.

But comparisons are detrimental to your marriage for three reasons.

First, and most important, comparisons fuel dissatisfaction. You develop "mate envy" or "life envy," and feel increasingly dissatisfied with your circumstances. You engage in "comparison shopping," wanting to make sure you're getting a good deal. Problem is, you can always find someone who seems to have it better—because what's new and untested always looks like an improvement to what you have. You imagine how much better others have it. The attractive, intense, romantic heartthrobs in the novels you read leave you unsatisfied with the level of romance in your marriage. The lavish lifestyle of a friend makes you feel discontented with your mate's contribution to the family budget.

Second, comparisons keep us focused on the negative. Analyzing the habits, appearance, or personality of your spouse can result in a critical spirit toward them. It also negates their positive qualities and contributions to the relationship.

Third, comparisons keep us living in unreality. Every marriage has issues. When you compare your mate to that of another, you are doing so from a distance. This distance allows you to create all kinds of illusions in your head for what life is like with a different partner. These illusions can be so tempting that they seem real. But every couple has their own set of problems they need to work out. What looks idyllic or preferable to you may be very different in reality. Living in reality and letting go of comparisons is vital to sustaining the positive mindset necessary to a growing marriage.

Here's a strategy for letting go of comparisons: write down all the positive qualities you see in your spouse. If the list is short, look back on your relationship and the contributions your mate has made to your life and to the family. Ruminate on their positive qualities. Post the list where you can see it and add to it regularly. Every day, look for one positive thing about your mate. And let them know what you see. This refocusing will allow you to feel more gratitude, which will relieve the temptation to compare.

Let Go of Demands

A demand is an attempt to get from our mate what we think we need. When we fear our needs won't be met, we become anxious or angry and insist our mate give us what we require. We think if we put our foot down hard enough that our needs will be satisfied. We hope, by so doing, that they will not only comply but see the rightness of the demand. We hope to compel them to do the *right* thing.

At the core of such a demand is the belief that our mate has the power to make us happy or unhappy. If I demand that my husband sweep the patio a certain way, I must believe that if he doesn't do so my happiness will be seriously thwarted. If you're married to someone who likes to please others to avoid conflict, your demand may get you a tidy patio but you will end up with a resentful partner.

However, I might desire he do it in a certain way—and I could request it. A request is much different than a demand. It doesn't carry the sense of ultimatum that characterizes a demand. A demand would say, "You need to sweep like this," or "You call that sweeping the patio?" A request says, "I'd really appreciate it if you could get all the leaves when you sweep the patio."

James and Amy struggled with demands. Amy lost her cool when James had to spend long hours at work, leaving her to eat dinner alone once or twice a week. When they arrived at my office for therapy, Amy's face was flushed with frustration and anger. James plopped into the corner of the sofa.

"So, I can see things are pretty heated right now," I said. "Who'd like to begin?"

"We got in a fight on the way here," James grumbled.

"He just doesn't get it!" Amy choked out, clearly trying to contain herself. "All day I look forward to talking over dinner. But he just blows it off!"

"I'm not blowing it off. I have a lot of extra work right now. There's no one else who can do it."

"So tell your boss to hire another person."

"I can't do that. He's already stressed out about our sales numbers being down."

Amy crossed her arms. "Apparently you care more about him than me. Either you get home on time for dinner or don't bother coming home at all!"

James turned to me. "See how unreasonable she is? She's never had a job in tech. She doesn't know how it is."

I focused first on Amy. "I can see how much pain you are in at not being able to count on spending time with your husband at dinner each night." Then I addressed James. "I can also see how difficult this is for you, trying to meet your job requirements and also be there for Amy." I leaned back and looked at both of them. "What if we could help your protective parts not react so strongly? Then, no matter what the other person says or does, you can stay centered and have more choices about how to respond."[2]

"Yes, please," said Amy.

"I guess," said James.

For the remainder of the session I coached James and Amy to talk about their emotions and their fears. Amy felt hurt, sad, and abandoned by her husband's frequent absences. Her protector tried to ensure she was cared for by challenging James's commitment to her and criticizing his priorities. James felt stressed and frustrated by what he perceived as Amy's unreasonableness. After attempts to explain his situation failed, his protector tried to prevent further stress by shutting down.

As this couple began to explore their own protectors—the roles they played and the fears that drove them—they were able to discover the young, vulnerable parts in themselves and each other that these protectors were guarding. As each told their story of childhood wounding, they began to feel a deep sense of compassion for the other. Amy's longing for connection with her unavailable parents made total sense to James. And once Amy understood James's experience of forbidden emotions, a light went on for her.

Amy gazed into James's eyes. "I can see how my anger and my demand that you tell your boss what to do might cause you stress."

"I'll do everything I can do to be home on time," James said. "Would it work for you if I make it home for dinner, then got in an hour of work time after?"

Amy considered his idea. "I'm okay with that. And it's all right if you need to stay late once in a while. I just need to know you want to be with me."

"Of course I do."

As Amy expressed her desires in a less demanding, less volatile way, James became empathetic and reassuring. At the conclusion of the session, they felt they were on the same team, trying together to manage the heightened stress of James's job.

There may be situations that compel you to set strong boundaries with your mate. If they are abusive or have been unfaithful, or if they have unsafe habits or addictions, you need to be very firm about what you will and will not tolerate. But even in these situations demands typically backfire. Instead make a firm and enforceable statement about your boundaries and what you need to stay in the relationship. Your own self-respect is a powerful boundary.

Consider your typical communication with your spouse. The last few times you asked your mate to do something, did you use the language of demand or request? Consider how you could have expressed your desire as a request rather than a demand. Practice saying it. The next time you want something from your mate, try to state it as a desire. They will feel more respected and will likely be more responsive.

Let Go of Resentment

Couples often find it difficult to move toward a more intimate relationship because they are nursing old wounds. Earlier in your relationship, your spouse may have hurt you in some way. Perhaps he failed to be there for you when you needed him. Perhaps she said or did something disrespectful to you. Perhaps he betrayed you in some way that cut you to your core.

You may have been hurt, neglected, criticized, dismissed, or shamed in your childhood. You may have suffered the withdrawal of a parent's love or the inconsistent presence of one or both parents. You may have been conditioned to believe your parents' love was based on how well you performed. Few people leave childhood unscathed. Most of us carry injuries that, if unidentified and unresolved, will get triggered when our spouse behaves in certain ways.

Few people leave childhood unscathed. Most of us carry injuries that, if unidentified and unresolved, will get triggered when our spouse behaves in certain ways.

Your hurt may stem from a one-time incident that has been difficult to forgive. It may also be the result of a long-standing pattern of behavior that causes ongoing damage. Over time resentment builds, creating a wall between you and your spouse.

Most couples are unaware how injuries from childhood feed their bitterness. They hold their mate fully to blame and resist any suggestion that they might have earlier wounds that create vulnerabilities to their mate's behavior. Feeling unsafe, they nurse their wounds and guard their hearts.

Resentment protects you by not allowing your mate to get close enough to inflict any more injury. It becomes leverage to ensure your safety. The idea of letting go of it may feel scary.

Resentfulness carries an element of anger—anger toward your spouse who wounded you, anger that they have not paid sufficiently for their offense. You may fear your spouse may get away with what they did or repeat their behavior if you don't stand watch over the trove of resentment. Not wanting your spouse to make light of your pain, you hold on to your resentment as if it alone validates your experience.

If you have been hurt by your spouse, your attempts to protect yourself from further pain are understandable and valid. However, holding on to your resentment will not accomplish what you desire: a safe and loving relationship with your spouse.

To be known, loved, and protected in your marriage, you need to become aware of the ways in which you are protecting yourself. As you come to appreciate what your resentful part has been doing to ensure your safety, you can invite that part to step down and let you tap into the courage to risk again.

Share with your spouse what you notice yourself doing to protect your heart from being hurt. Tell them what they did that triggered a wound from childhood. Ask them to help you take down the wall so the two of you can become close once again. Share with your spouse what you need to feel safe. If your mate continues in a pattern of hurt, communicate the boundaries you need to set in order to protect yourself.

It may be helpful to process your feelings with a mentor, friend, pastor, or therapist.

To move forward, you need to face your fears and risk letting your spouse into your circle of trust. No human is fully trustworthy in the sense that they will never fail or hurt you. We all "stumble in many ways," as the Bible reminds us (James 3:2). There are no guarantees you won't be hurt in the future. But you won't enjoy the potential of growing love in your relationship if you refuse to forgive your imperfectly loving mate.

Let Go of Shame

Steve was feeling a huge weight of shame when he and Jill first arrived in my office. He had been unemployed for ten months and felt he had let the family down. Shame had given way to depression, which further immobilized him in his struggle to find work. Whenever Jill prodded him to look more aggressively, he reacted with anger. Jill had no awareness that Steve was burdened with shame, as she only saw his angry or lethargic sides.

Matt had dealt with a huge weight of guilt. While dating Kim, he had fallen in love with Stacey. He continued dating Kim, in case the relationship with Stacey didn't work out. Matt felt guilty about his duplicity but couldn't figure out how to break the news to Kim. His guilt eventually led him to come clean with Stacey, which led to a huge blowup. The next day, he ended his relationship with Kim.

Shame and guilt are different experiences. Shame says, "I am bad," "I am not enough," or "I am too much." Guilt, on the other hand, says "I *did* something wrong." Guilt can prompt us to do the right thing or weigh us down until we decide to admit or rectify the situation. Healthy guilt calls us into more honest, transparent living.

Shame, on the other hand, keeps us stuck, believing we are bad and unworthy. Shame is a belief we have about ourselves at the core. Researcher Brene Brown defines shame as "the intensely painful feeling or experience of believing we are flawed and therefore unworthy of acceptance and belonging."[3]

Shame is often the result of messages we've received from others and internalized. As children, we may have been criticized or told we were bad or incapable by a parent or teacher. When we are made to feel like we are not enough or too much, we feel shame.

To push away the feeling of shame, we develop ways of protecting ourselves—including getting angry, blaming others, hiding our vulnerabilities, or even shaming ourselves. We develop an internal critic to keep ourselves in check and thereby avoid the shaming messages of others. What was once done to us we now do to ourselves.

Seth and Amber found themselves in a cycle of shame and blame. As Seth began to face the damaging effect of his anger on his wife and children, he connected to a deep reservoir of shame he had experienced since childhood. His revelation of his father's anger, and his genuine remorse for his own anger, moved Amber to compassion.

However, whenever Seth complained about Amber, she would counter with a direct or indirect reminder of his past offenses. This would cause him to go into punitive self-recriminations. Because of his past infractions, he felt he didn't deserve to have a complaint. So he allowed Amber to dismiss his concerns.

In therapy, Amber was able to see how her reaction triggered shame for Seth. And eventually, Seth saw how his self-blame got in the way of bringing his whole self to the relationship.

Letting go of shame is not easy. But exploring the messages you received early in life can help you see how you may have been shamed. Considering your own thought life, and noticing any critical or accusatory things you say to yourself about yourself, can also give you clues about the presence of shame.

Once you have identified your shamed parts, reflect on how you protect yourself from feeling shame. Noticing your own reactivity to others—such as anger and blame—can help detect the protectors you have developed.

Having compassion for those shamed parts of yourself is an important step toward healing and allowing yourself to respond more calmly when you receive a hurtful message from your mate. Let that young part of you that received damaging messages as a child know you see and understand their pain. Remind them they are "wonderfully made" (Ps. 139:14) and that they have a divine

Parent who loves them unconditionally. Assure them of your intention to love them similarly.

You can also offer compassion to your protector parts that have been trying to shield you from further shame. Let them know you appreciate their efforts and invite them to step back and trust you with your interactions with your spouse and others. Knowing our internal parts that hold shame and protect us from it is important to letting go of shame and entering into more loving ways of being with ourselves and our mate.

It takes a great deal of courage to let go of strategies and beliefs that have helped you make sense of your world and your relationships. Hanging on to old patterns of negative interpretations, mindreading, or demanding may give you a sense of security, but it won't take you where you want to go. In the words of Helen Keller, "Security is mostly a superstition. Life is either a daring adventure or nothing."[4]

Releasing these old strategies, and the beliefs that support them, allows you to receive your mate in a healthier way and invite new awareness into your marriage. It allows both of you to explore each other's complexities, and it frees you from patterns that have hindered the love you long for.

Discussion Questions: Chapter 7

Group and Couple Questions

Have each person go through the "For Personal Reflection" questions below before you gather together.

1. Why is it so tempting to think you can read your mate's mind or motives? Why is this counterproductive? Describe a time when you attempted to mind-read only to discover that your interpretation was incorrect. How does it feel when others misread your thoughts or intentions? Read Matthew 7:1–5. What do these verses say about judging your mate's motives?

2. What is the difference between a demand and a request? When someone approaches you with a need, would you like them to do so with a demand or a request? What feels disrespectful about a demand?

3. Read Ephesians 4:2, 31–32; Proverbs 14:30; and Galatians 6:4. What is the relationship between humility and mindreading, negative interpretations, and unreasonable expectations? How do comparisons lead to envy? How is forgiveness an antidote to resentment? Share one thing you are willing to let go of to improve your relationship with your spouse.

4. Share your primary takeaway from your personal reflections (below).

For Personal Reflection

1. What is something you need to let go of to improve communication or enhance intimacy with your mate? What has been difficult about letting it go? Can you identify the belief you hold that keeps you holding on to the pattern or behavior?

2. Do you ever find yourself making assumptions about your mate's thoughts or intentions? Have you ever had the experience of believing you know what they are thinking and disputing any explanation they offer? What will be hard about letting go of the temptation to mind-read or make assumptions? Next time you are inclined to jump to a conclusion or make an assumption, check it out with your mate. Ask them to clarify. You might ask, "Can you help me understand what you were thinking?"

3. Have you caught yourself interpreting your mate's behavior in a consistently negative light? Try asking yourself, *Is there any possibility that I'm seeing this incorrectly?* Give yourself room to be wrong. If your mate's positive or neutral

behavior is regularly seen as negative, they will become disillusioned.

4. Think of the expectation you have of your mate that causes the most disappointment for you. Ask yourself where this expectation came from. Is there a fear involved? What would happen if your mate didn't come through for you in the way you expect? What would that say about you? What gets triggered in you at the thought of not having things as you wish they were? Exploring the fears underlying your expectations or perfectionism is helpful in allowing you to shift the focus from your mate to your own protectors. Doing so will increase your self-awareness and help you let go and shift to more reasonable expectations.

5. Do you find yourself comparing your mate to the mates of others? Write down all the positive qualities you see in your mate. Look back on your relationship and the good contributions your mate has made to your life and to the family. Let yourself ruminate on their positive qualities. Post this list where you can read and add to it every day. Then, each day, coach yourself to look for one positive thing about your mate and let them know what you see.

6. The last few times you have asked your mate to do something, have you used the language of demand or of desire? Reflect on what you might have said if you were to express the request as a desire rather than a demand. Practice saying it. Next time you have a request of your mate, intentionally state it as a desire.

7. Have you been feeling resentful toward your spouse? Ask yourself what longing you have that is not being met. Is the longing connected to anything from your childhood? Think about your resentment as a part of you (it's not all of you) that has a role in protecting you from the hurt of that unmet longing. As you notice what your resentful part

has been doing in an attempt to get what you desire, offer it some appreciation. Then invite that part to step down and let you tap into the courage to risk again.

You might share with your spouse what you notice you have been doing to protect yourself from hurt. You might share with them what they did to hurt you and what it triggered from your childhood. You might ask them if they could help you take down the wall so you can once again become close. Share with them what you need to feel safe or loved.

8. Consider your own thought life and notice any critical or accusing things you say to yourself about yourself. Once you have identified your shamed parts, reflect on how you protect yourself from feeling shame. (Noticing your own reactivity to others is a way to detect the protectors you have developed against experiencing shame—anger, blame, and so forth.)

Extend compassion to those shamed parts of yourself. Let that young part of you that received shaming messages as a child know you see and understand their pain. Remind them that they are "wonderfully made" (Ps. 139:14) and that they have a divine Parent who loves them unconditionally. Assure them of your intention to learn to love them similarly.

Offer compassion to your protector parts that have been trying to protect you from further shame by reacting defensively (through anger, withdrawal, and so forth). Let them know you appreciate their efforts and invite them to step back and trust you with your interactions with your spouse and others.

8

Lean In

It's those little moments that you rarely think about—when you're shopping at the supermarket, folding laundry, or having a quickie catch-up call while you're both still at work—that make up the heart and soul of a marriage.

John Gottman

Life happens. Work piles up, finances get tight, kids act up. In the midst of the stresses and strains of life, your attention is redirected toward the urgent needs—and your marriage can suffer. The daily grind chips away at the connection you used to share. How do you navigate the ebbs and flows of life as a team? What keeps you together as waves of responsibility and demands, inside and outside the home, clamor for your attention?

It's not the big vacations or extravagant gifts or romantic events that cement the connection of a thriving marriage. It is the small increments of behavior that make the difference. A wife asks her husband to pick up the laundry on his way home and he responds, "Sure," instead of pretending he didn't hear. A wife senses her husband's stress and sends him a funny text at work. Little acts of connection that nourish love.

Every moment you share with your spouse, you either lean in to the relationship or lean out. When your spouse makes a bid for your attention or affection and you respond positively, you nourish connection. Your mate feels noticed, considered, and valued. When you lean out, you create distance that, over time, negatively affects the relationship. Becoming aware of and acting on these opportunities is necessary to nurturing a loving relationship.

It's not the big vacations or extravagant gifts or romantic events that cement the connection of a thriving marriage. It is the small increments of behavior that make the difference.

Researcher John Gottman compares the things couples do to remain emotionally engaged or to distance themselves to having an "emotional bank account."[1] He suggests that partners who respond positively to their mate's bids for attention, affection, humor, or support are putting money in their marriage's emotional bank. When difficult times come, due to life's changes, stress, or hardship, couples who have invested in their relationship weather these challenges far better than those who have neglected to put regular deposits in the bank.

Our neglect of our marriage is not intentional, at least at first. Over time we become preoccupied with other concerns and priorities, and our mate takes a back burner. We get caught up in what we perceive has to be done and assume our mate will be available when we make the turn and move in their direction. We take them for granted and then often find this depletion in the emotional bank account has taken its toll. Our spouse may feel resentful, neglected, or otherwise unavailable if the account has suffered from too many withdrawals.

If you are suffering from a depleted emotional bank account, or if you want to continue to invest in your account and keep those dividends flowing, you need to be intentional. To love proactively, rather than passively, requires you to make a conscious decision to move toward your mate.

Think of leaning in to your marriage as a daily habit, like brushing your teeth or checking your email. In time, the things you do to enrich your relationship will become so habitual you won't even have to think about them. They will become part of the DNA of your marriage.

Most habits that replenish a relationship only take a moment—giving your mate a word of appreciation or kissing them goodbye. Others will involve a bit more thought—planning a birthday surprise or date night. Some involve a word spoken, and others are expressed nonverbally. Anything you do that leans toward your mate and conveys "I care" is a point of connection.

Appreciation

We all like to feel appreciated. It tells us that what we have to bring to the relationship is noticed and valued. A simple word of appreciation can go a long way toward reducing stress and helping our mate calm internally. It also benefits us to focus on what we are grateful for.

In a National Institutes of Health study, researchers examined how blood flow in different regions of the brain is affected by a person's feeling of gratitude.[2] They found that subjects who showed more gratitude had higher levels of activity in the hypothalamus, which controls sleep, body temperature, metabolism, hunger, and stress levels. That higher activity level means reduced stress and improved sleep, benefiting our experience of well-being.

Appreciation is also great for a marriage.

Nick routinely brings the trash cans in after garbage pickup day. When he walks in from the garage, Jennifer says, "Thank you for bringing those cans in. I really appreciate it." Nick's rough day at work just got a little lighter.

Jill gives Steve a call during the day to let him know that she is going to pick up dinner on the way home, so she might be a bit later than usual. When she gets home, Steve says, "Thanks for picking up dinner." Glad to know that her efforts are noticed, Jill feels more warmly toward Steve.

A simple "Thanks, honey" or "I appreciate you" communicated in a note, over the phone, or face-to-face creates an aura of good feeling that can permeate all other interactions. Regular expressions of gratefulness for your partner's efforts or character will sustain a sense of connection, even when you and your mate are apart.

Commit yourself to daily expressing to your mate one quality or action you are grateful for. After a week, notice the deeper sense of connection you feel.

One additional benefit of gratefulness: it releases dopamine, a neurotransmitter in the brain that triggers feelings of pleasure or reward. Dopamine urges us to repeat the behavior to enjoy additional pleasure. Gratefulness produces more gratefulness—a great ongoing recipe for marital happiness!

Affirmation

An affirmation is a statement to your mate of your admiration for who they are and what they bring to life. It focuses on their character rather than their actions or behavior. It is a declaration of what you treasure about your mate.

Affirmations express recognition of your mate's created essence. Author John Powell stated, "It is an absolute human certainty that no one can know his own beauty or perceive a sense of his own worth until it has been reflected back to him in the mirror of another loving, caring human being."[3] Affirmations provide that reflection.

To tell your mate, "You are strong in the ways that are important to me" or "I love how you are so playful with the kids" connects with the core of their sense of self. It affirms them in deep and meaningful ways. It is about *who* they are.

Think of the three things you admire most about your spouse. Put each of these thoughts into a sentence that captures how you feel. Then share one each week for the next three weeks. Notice how simply thinking about affirmations changes how you feel about your mate. Continue to offer at least one affirmation every week. You could also sit down with your spouse and come up with five marriage affirmations each, then combine your lists into one and post it in several places in your home. A marriage affirmation might be something like "We give each other room to make mistakes" or "We enjoy walking together after dinner." Take time each week to read them and check in with each other on how you're doing at living out your affirmations.

Partings and Greetings

For most couples, workdays involve one or both of you leaving home in the morning and returning at night. These points of parting and reuniting provide important moments that can connect you or create more distance. Couples whose schedules or moods cause them to neglect their goodbyes and hellos end up drifting apart.

James and Amy found themselves sliding toward disconnection. James's schedule required him to leave the house at 6:45 a.m., and Amy didn't leave till 7:15. Amy was usually in the shower when James left for work, and they had fallen into the habit of not connecting in the morning. They went about their day focused on their own concerns. When James returned from work, Amy was home but preoccupied. When she heard him walk in, she hoped he would come and find her, but he typically sat in the kitchen until she came out. When she did come into the kitchen, their greeting was cordial but lacked enthusiasm.

In therapy, after we discussed the importance of them connecting at the beginning of the day, James and Amy made a point of kissing each other goodbye and asking each other to share one thing they were anticipating or dreading about their day. Sometimes it was an important meeting or a difficult conversation. Other times it was a fun lunch with a coworker or an expected errand. Just knowing something about how each other would be spending their day allowed them to feel more connected. When they returned at night, James sought out Amy and gave her a kiss hello. Over dinner they checked in with each other about how their anticipated event had gone. This provided a way for each to express interest and care about the daily life of the other. After a few weeks, James and Amy felt much closer.

If you've been letting your partings and greetings slide, consider reinstating them. Those simple hello and goodbye kisses will vitalize your marriage and help you and your spouse stay connected even when you're apart.

Nurturing Shared Interests

You've probably heard that "opposites attract." It's true that we usually marry people who are different from us. We look for mates who complement us because they have something we don't, and vice versa. Therefore, couples usually have different interests.

My husband loves fly-fishing. I love being outdoors, but spending nine hours cramped on a small fishing boat covered with bugs is not my idea of a good day. I love water sports. When he's not in a boat, my husband is a landlubber. Over the years, we have learned to lean in to each other's interests. I'll go fly-fishing for half a day. My husband will snorkel with me when we take trips to tropical spots.

My husband loves watching me catch a fish on a fly rod. To him, it's sexy. Go figure.

Leaning in to your mate's interests is a gift to them and to yourself. It stretches you and allows your spouse to enjoy your presence while they pursue their interests.

This is not to say you can't enjoy certain activities that are not shared by your partner. You just need to share some activities together. And the activities you don't share should be limited so they don't drain off marital synergy.

Sometimes one person's interest can become a shared one. When I joined a women's cycling group, I had to train every Saturday morning for three months. That was a big sacrifice, as my husband and I had always shared Saturdays as a couple. By the end of the first month, he was unhappy with our lack of time together. At that point, he had a choice. He could ask me to give up my new hobby or he could figure out a way to participate. He decided to become the team videographer, coming out on Saturdays to film us on our rides. How sweet is that? The other cyclists got their own copies of the video at the team party at the conclusion of the training. My husband was a hit with the team and with me. Subsequently, we bought him a bike, and now he and I enjoy cycling as a couple on the weekends.

There are many things you can enjoy together. Going to movies, dining out, playing games. Perhaps you can take a dance, exercise, or art class together. Find good hikes in your area, take a Sunday drive, or volunteer together. Whatever your differing interests, you can always nourish a shared one.

Try this. Sit down together and each write down ten activities you enjoy. Rate them from one to ten based on your level of enjoyment, ten being highest. Share your lists. If there are any interests you both enjoy, highlight those. If any items on your mate's list are not on yours, and you would be willing to try them, put an X next to them. Then make a plan together to invest time in the highlighted activities and consider how you might also prioritize the items marked with an X.

Laughing Together

When was the last time you had a good laugh with your spouse? There's nothing quite like the bonding power of a good laugh. Most of us encounter a good deal of stress in our daily lives, which tends to make us overly serious. We lose our sense of humor, and with it our resiliency as a couple.

Whether stresses originate from a job or the challenges of balancing kids, home maintenance, or other responsibilities, they often lead to marital tension. When stress is activated the body continuously releases cortisol, chronic elevated levels of which can lead to serious problems. Too much cortisol can suppress the immune system, increase blood pressure and sugar, contribute to obesity, and more.

What's a proven antidote for stress? Laughter.

A study of sixty women was conducted in 2015 at the ASAN Medical Center on the use of laughter as a therapy in coping with breast cancer.[4] The researchers found that laughter was effective in reducing anxiety, depression, and stress in breast cancer patients. Other studies have demonstrated major positive effects on quality of life, resilience, immunity, and insomnia in cancer patients.[5] Laughter is just good for you.

One way to increase the laughter quotient in your marriage is to let yourselves be silly. Friends of ours created a wonderfully playful memory while on a cruise. Cruise ships have all sorts of nooks and crannies. When Tom looked at Barb with a mischievous grin and said, "If I catch ya, I'm gonna have to kill ya," the game was on!

Barb darted off and Tom was in hot pursuit. She would dodge into a corner and when she saw him run by, she'd peel out and head the other direction. Soon fellow passengers were peeking up from their activities and asking what was happening. To their strange looks, they would both explain, "We're playing chase." The onlookers quickly took interest and would say to Tom, "She went that way," or to Barb, "Get out of here!"

At one point, when he was running up a stairway, Tom grabbed a woman's leg that looked an awful lot like Barb's. Much to his surprise and hers, it belonged to another.

After an hour of fun, Tom spotted Barb through the windows at the back of the ship. She saw him and ran for "safety," but chose the wrong direction and was caught. They collapsed in laughter. What began with a moment of mischief had brought hilarity to their relationship and their new friends onboard!

My favorite family vacation tradition is to surprise my kids with a spontaneous water balloon fight. Invariably, other vacationers join in on the hilarity. Great fun!

A wonderful way to enjoy laughter with your spouse is to develop an inside joke. My husband was once given a birthday card that showed an old couple looking out across a body of water toward a peninsula. The picture on the front of the card showed the wife asking her husband what the narrow stretch of land was called. Not knowing, he concocted an answer and confidently said, "It's a stick out." The inside of the card read, "One year older, and one year closer to making up bunk." Now, whenever my husband and I encounter someone we think is making something up, we look at each other and whisper, "Stick out!" It always brings a smile to our faces.

Laughter has a way of relieving stress and reminding us to enjoy our mate. Famed comedian Bob Hope said laughter is an "instant vacation." It relaxes us and reminds us that there's joy even in the mundane moments of life. A steady diet of humor will go a long way toward giving your relationship the elasticity it needs for the two of you to stay connected, even in the midst of challenges.

A steady diet of humor will go a long way toward giving your relationship the elasticity it needs for the two of you to stay connected, even in the midst of challenges.

Physical Touch

Research consistently reveals that the value of touch in the life of a growing child cannot be underestimated. Touch communicates that the child is valued, wanted, safe, and loved. The same is true for adults. We never outgrow our need for physical touch. Respected family therapist Virginia Satir once said, "We need four hugs a day for survival. We need eight hugs a day for maintenance. We need twelve hugs a day for growth."[6] Physical connection is crucial to our well-being.

In marriage, we have the delightful opportunity to give that touch to our mate. Holding hands, hugging, massaging, kissing, and embracing all communicate, "You are important to me, you are loved, and I care."

Physical touch also has physiological benefits. Our skin has receptors beneath the surface that, when touched, lower our blood pressure and cortisol levels, which in turn reduces our stress.

A study of sixty women conducted at the University of North Carolina found that women who hugged their partners frequently (even for just twenty seconds) had lower blood pressure and heart rate, which decreases the risk of cardiovascular disease, and higher levels of oxytocin.[7] Oxytocin, a "bonding hormone," makes people feel secure and trusting toward each other, lowers cortisol levels, and reduces stress. Touch is fundamental to human communication, bonding, and health.[8]

To increase the physical touch in your relationship, sit down with your spouse and write down the top five ways you each like to receive touch. Perhaps your mate enjoys a warm hug, holding hands, or a back rub. Maybe what feels good to you is an arm around your waist, a foot massage, or cuddling on the sofa. Write out your preferences and share them with each other. Then commit yourself to offering your mate one item on their list each day.

If you are uncomfortable with physical touch, it is likely you grew up in a home without much affectionate contact. This will be a growth area for you. Rather than rebuffing touch because of the discomfort, coach yourself to receive touch as a signal that you are loved and valued by your mate. Share with your mate what is most comfortable to you, then stretch to those areas that are less comfortable. This will help you grow physically closer to your spouse.

Compromise

Compromise can be viewed as a path to achieving a shared goal or as capitulation that diminishes individuality and freedom of choice. Matt and Stacey found it difficult to sacrifice their own needs and wants for the sake of the other or their relationship. When they met, they had each fashioned their own careers, created their own living spaces, and cultivated their own friendships. Neither felt inclined to sacrifice their desires to accommodate the relationship.

They frequently fought about who had to give up what in order to merge their lives. Matt insisted on continuing his frequent outings with the guys, even during seasons when Stacey traveled a lot and had limited time to be with him. Deciding whose apartment to move into became a competitive argument, with neither wanting to give up his or her turf. One of the most difficult discussions came over the guest list for the wedding.

A huge argument had ensued the day before their visit to my office. As they entered, Matt was tense, his face flushed, and Stacey was clearly frustrated. They each took a seat on opposite ends of the sofa, as if to declare their unwillingness to move toward center.

"I can sense tension in both of you," I said. "Who would like to start?"

"I will," Matt said. He clearly wanted to plead his case. "Stacey is so unreasonable. She has invited her entire family to our wedding, even cousins and second cousins. I've never met half of these people. If they're so important to her, why hasn't she ever mentioned them to me?"

"You invited your entire family," Stacey said. "Why can't I invite all of mine?"

"Because your family is twice as big! It's going to be too crazy expensive." Matt turned to me. "Besides, she refuses to let me invite all of my buddies."

"You've already invited twenty," Stacey said.

"Just because you don't have as many friends as I do, that doesn't mean I should have to eliminate some of mine."

"Maybe we should just cancel the wedding." Stacey teared up. "I can't stand all this arguing."

I invited Matt and Stacey to identify the feelings they were experiencing as they thought about the wedding list. Matt said he noticed some tension in his stomach that he felt sure was related to the cost. He expressed fear and anxiety about the burden of wedding debt. He also felt some anger toward Stacey, whom he felt was dismissive of his concerns.

Stacey identified a feeling of pressure in her chest. She felt caught between Matt and her parents, who valued extended family connection and had expressed a desire for the wedding to be a reunion of the clan. She was also angry with Matt for what she perceived as his valuing of friends over family.

As we talked further, it became clear that Matt's concern about the financial aspect of the wedding had a history. He described his dad, an accountant, as frugal and a good money manager. He had done well in life financially, and Matt was determined to follow in his footsteps. Stacey's concern about inviting the whole family to the wedding also had a history. Her relatives, a tight Italian group, considered family to have priority over every other loyalty. Inviting the whole clan to events was a matter of course, and Stacey did not want to be the first to break with that tradition. The emotional price tag would be too high.

When Matt and Stacey expressed their feelings and fears, they felt more compassion for each other's viewpoint. They knew they needed to compromise to be able to move forward. Stacey agreed to trim her list to some degree as long as Matt was willing to run interference with her family if they gave her any grief. Matt agreed to stretch the budget enough to include a dozen of Stacey's "second tier" relatives and also to work with her to reduce costs in other areas of the wedding budget.

These compromises were made possible by a new awareness of two important factors: their positions were derived from their family histories and their self-protective stances were caused by underlying fear. The impasse shifted from one spouse being right and the other being wrong to mutual understanding and working together to find a solution.

In every good marriage, each spouse needs to bend and, on occasion, give up his or her own desires or position for the sake of the marriage. For those who are fiercely independent, or who built a life of their own before marrying, this can be difficult. "Merger marriages" tend to have more problems with compromise than "start-up marriages." But because all marriages are made up of two individuals who are different, compromise is the best way to move forward, making important life decisions together. You each learn to give something up in order to get something greater: intimate companionship and a shared life, which will shape you both into more loving, less self-absorbed people.

Apologizing

Nobody likes to be wrong. Being right feels a lot better. When we were children, doing the right thing usually got us approval and praise, or at least helped us avoid criticism for doing something bad. We came to equate being wrong with punishment or the withdrawal of a parent's affections. To avoid this, we learned how to defend ourselves and justify our behavior.

As a result, apologizing to our mate is not typically our go-to reflex. We are much more inclined to defend and excuse ourselves. Even if we do apologize, it is often couched in terms that avoid full responsibility. "I'm sorry you feel that way" avoids any ownership of wrongdoing. The mate on the receiving end of that statement usually feels dismissed.

Our apologies are also usually couched in some kind of excuse. "I'm sorry, *but* I had a lot on my plate today" feels more like an evasion than a sincere apology. Since we don't want to take full responsibility or look like the bad guy, we respond in a way that dismisses our spouse's complaints and minimizes our accountability.

Often our resistance to offering an apology is fueled by our suddenly heightened awareness of our mate's faults and mistakes. We think if we apologize then their failings will go unnoticed or be deemed as less important than our own. In our rationalizing, we shift the blame to their offenses.

Just the other day, my husband pointed out that I had dismissed his concern. In that moment, I was conveniently reminded of how he had done the same just a few days earlier. I reminded him of his infraction. This did nothing to repair our relationship.

We all make mistakes. We're all prone to do things that hurt or frustrate our mate. When we do, a sincere apology is the most effective way to repair a break in the relationship and restore connection. An apology done well is a powerful tool that can restore a marriage.

Here are the ingredients of an effective, heartfelt apology:

1. *Search yourself.* Before you approach your mate, take some time to consider whether you have any self-protective parts that want to minimize or defend the offense. We are all vulnerable to rationalizations, so be brutally honest with yourself. Imagine being on the receiving end of what you did and the hurt it may have caused.

2. *Admit it.* Your offense may be minor, such as forgetting to put something on your calendar or failing to run an errand. Or it might be big, such as betraying a trust or hiding an addiction. Admitting involves acknowledging your fault without minimizing its impact or excusing yourself in any way. When you admit your wrongdoing, be specific. A vague apology is cowardly and not nearly as reparative as a detailed one that clearly states what occurred.

3. *Acknowledge hurt.* Try to understand and empathize with the pain you have caused. Ask your mate what feelings came up for them when you did what you did. Let them know that it makes sense to you that they would feel what they felt (hurt, disappointed, frustrated, and so forth).

4. *Accept the consequences.* If the offense causes your mate to withdraw for a while, allow that time without demanding that they instantly forgive. If the offense is big and has wounded a core part of your mate, let them know you understand their need for time and that you will be patient. Check in occasionally and find out if they need anything from you to soothe the hurt.

5. *Alter your behavior.* Changing how you treat your mate is evidence that you have taken your offense seriously and sincerely desire to love them better. Altering behavior is a sign that your heart was engaged in the apology.[9]

In most situations, each of you holds some responsibility for what happened. You cannot apologize for your mate's side of things but you can fully own your side without expecting a reciprocated apology from your mate. Apologies are unilateral—they involve an admission of your part in the conflict. If you demand that your mate own their part as a condition for offering yours, the apology is not sincere. Your mate may need time to get their protectors to step down before they can acknowledge their part. Give them that time. It is more important that an apology be sincere than it be extracted from an unwilling spouse.

Forgiving

When we are hurt, it is natural to want to protect ourselves from further pain. We guard our wounds and suspect our mate's intentions. We hesitate or refuse to offer forgiveness. We fear that if we forgive our mate, either the behavior will be repeated and/or they won't take their offenses seriously. We want them to feel the sting of our distance in order to convey the severity of their offense. We don't want them to minimize or excuse what they've done.

When our mate wounds us, we think they owe us something. An apology would be nice—a guarantee or promise never to do it again even nicer. Most often, this desire to extract something from our mate is a product of our pride. They have done something to hurt us, and we feel slighted.[10] We want to defend our image and not let our mate off the hook with any premature forgiveness. We refuse to lift the sanctions until they have sufficiently paid for their offense. Refusing to pardon allows us to keep the powerful cards in our hands until our ego is soothed.

In protecting ourselves and withholding forgiveness, however, we contribute to the lack of safety in the relationship. If your partner can't mess up without incurring prolonged disconnection from you, they will learn to hide themselves and erect their own barriers to protect themselves from you.

Failing to forgive is a form of judgment. It says, "You are not worthy of a second chance or my trust." It judges the mate's lapse in behavior as a major defect in character.

Withholding forgiveness suggests that we are blind to our own imperfections and hurtful ways.[11] When we see our faults clearly, we have a better vantage point to see our mate's flaws. When we show a willingness to extend forgiveness, our spouse will likely be more forthright about their responsibility in hurting us.

Someone who is well aware of the way their protectors react, and the hurt they can inflict, tends to be a more gracious forgiver than a person who doesn't see their own responsibility. When partners forgive generously, the relationship becomes more authentic. Each can be who they truly are and know when they blow it, the other will still love them and not withdraw.

When you forgive your mate, you are not minimizing or excusing what they have done. You are saying, "What you did was wrong, but I am choosing to cancel the debt you owe me. I will no longer hold it against you."

Some people, particularly those who are compelled to please others, may ignore the harm done to them and call it forgiveness. Ignoring out of a fear of conflict, or a fear of being disconnected from the other if the offense were faced honestly, is not forgiveness or love. It is a lack of courage that will not benefit either the wounded or the offender. It is far more helpful to identify the behavior that caused the hurt and seek repair.

When partners forgive generously, the relationship becomes more authentic. Each can be who they truly are and know when they blow it, the other will still love them and not withdraw.

Nor is forgiveness merely the act of saying, "I forgive you." Forgiveness involves a change of heart toward the offender. It says, "What you did hurt me and I forgive you. I will not hold it against you or let it color how I see you in any way." It involves the complete surrender of the desire to get even.

Henri Nouwen is purported to have said, "Forgiveness is love practiced among people who love poorly." It must be practiced over and over again, since humans routinely fail to love. Forgiveness is a form of love that pursues the offender for the sake of restored relationship. To become a generous forgiver, you must allow yourself to be conscious of your own flaws and your need for forgiveness. And to see your mate as a work in progress, ever becoming that person God had in mind when he created them.

Forgiveness will often lead to reconciliation, as it releases the wrongdoer from any debt. Through forgiveness, the path to restoration of the relationship is made possible. There are, however, some situations in which forgiveness can take place without reconciliation—situations that remain unsafe (abuse) or where infidelity is taking place.

Forgiveness is not about condoning or going easy on injustice. Forgiveness in these instances is more about releasing the offender from any debt and giving up any need for retribution. It allows the forgiver to be free from ongoing anger, resentment, and negative thoughts. In most instances, however, forgiveness, even in situations of infidelity, can lead to reconciliation and a new quality of life together.

How do we go about forgiving our mate in a way that releases them from debt and paves the way for restoring the relationship? Here are four steps you can take:

1. *Search yourself.* Acknowledge any feelings that come up as a result of your partner's offense. Allow yourself to feel the pain, disrespect, fear, and so forth. Notice your protectors that get activated in an attempt to ensure your safety—anger, a desire to punish, or erecting an emotional wall.

2. *Engage your spouse.* Let your mate know what you are feeling and that you desire to forgive them. Be specific about your hurt and what you need in the future. Set any necessary boundaries that will protect the path of reconciliation (no name-calling, no late-night computer time, and so forth).

3. *Release.* Let go of negativity toward your partner. Relinquish blame, bitterness, resentment, and anger. Tim Keller offers this word on the release necessary in forgiveness: "One of the most basic skills in marriage is the ability to tell the straight, unvarnished truth about what your spouse has done—and then, completely, unself-righteously, and joyously express forgiveness without a shred of superiority, without making the other person feel small."[12] Releasing is about letting go of any need to hold the offense over your spouse, any need for retribution or payment.

   Assure whatever parts of you that may be fearful of future hurt that you are an adult and you will take care of yourself if and when that becomes necessary.

4. *Restore.* Tell your mate you forgive them. Invite them to help rebuild your lives together. Brainstorm, with each other, steps that will heal your marriage. If the infraction was small, it may be enough to plan a fun date on the weekend. If the offense was large, restoration may take weeks or months. Think about areas of reconnection, which may begin with shared activities such as holding hands or attending a marriage conference, and then advance to cuddling on the sofa, a weekend away, or getting silly together. Over time, you will likely enjoy a full repair that restores the vitality of your relationship.

Choosing to Lean

Changing marital habits takes conscious intentionality. Learning to lean in, to move toward your mate instead of away, is a choice you make every moment of your married life. Becoming more generous with your affirmations and appreciation will increase the fondness in your relationship and help you stay focused on why you said "I do."

New habits of parting and greeting and increased physical touch will help you feel connected throughout the day. Laughing together and developing enjoyable shared interests will reduce stress and deepen your marital friendship. Learning to more readily compromise, apologize, and forgive will allow you to resolve differences and repair hurt, thereby ensuring the elasticity your relationship needs to weather marital challenges.

Being proactive in instilling new habits will nourish that lifetime of love you desire. (For a summary of ideas about how to do that, see the "For Personal Reflection" section below.)

Discussion Questions: Chapter 8

Group Questions

Take time to do the "For Personal Reflection" and "Couple Exercises" sections before your group meeting.

1. Share your current habits of connection as a couple with the group. What are they? What do you notice specifically about the positive ways they impact your relationship? Read Philippians 2:3 and Romans 12:10. How might the attitudes expressed here help you lean in to your relationship?

2. Of the nine habits mentioned—appreciation, affirmation, partings and greetings, nurturing shared interests, laughing, physical touch, compromise, apologizing, and forgiving— which one do you have the most difficulty with as a couple? What gets in the way of developing this habit? Ask your group what they do that has been helpful in forming this habit.

3. Read Colossians 3:12–14. Discuss each quality mentioned and consider how "putting on" each one would change how you relate to your spouse in daily practical ways. Be specific.

4. Read James 5:16. Why is apologizing necessary?

5. Can you think of a time when you were forgiven? How did it feel? Read Ephesians 4:32; Luke 6:37–38; and Mark 11:25–26. What do these verses say about the relationship between forgiving and being forgiven by God? Are you a generous forgiver?

6. As a couple, decide three things you will do together to create a momentum of "leaning in" to your marriage by working on habits of connection. Come back to the group and share as many as you are comfortable, and invite the group to check back and see how you're doing.

For Personal Reflection

1. What are your current habits of connection? What feelings do they stir up as you engage in those habits?

2. *Appreciation*: commit yourself to daily expressing to your mate one quality or action that you are especially grateful for. After one week, notice the sense of connection you feel. Keep it going! For inspiration, read 1 Thessalonians 5:18.

3. *Affirmation*: think of the three things you admire most about your mate. Put each of these thoughts into a sentence that captures what you want to say. Then share one each week for the next three weeks. Make a plan to continue by offering one affirmation every week.

4. *Apologizing*: offer your mate a heartfelt apology for something you have done in the past month. Use the five-step process offered in the chapter. It's the first step to healing the relationship (James 5:16).

5. *Forgiving*: if your mate has offended or hurt you in some way, follow the steps to forgiveness outlined in the chapter to restore your relationship.

Couple Exercises

1. Separately, each make a list of the habits of connection you each currently enjoy, used to enjoy, and want to enjoy in the future. Share your lists with one another and make a composite list of the ones you want to integrate into the DNA of your relationship. Post the list in a place where you will read it daily.

2. *Partings and greetings*: make a commitment to bookend your day with kisses—when you leave in the morning, when you reunite in the evening, when you go to bed. Let your mate know that whatever happens those kisses will remain a part of your marital rituals.

Before you depart in the morning, check on one thing your mate has on their plate for the day. Remember to ask them about it when you come together at the end of the day. These small additions to your routine can revitalize your connection!

3. *Nurturing shared interests*: sit down together and each write down ten activities you enjoy. Then rate them from one to ten based on your level of enjoyment—ten being the one you like the most. Share your lists, and if there are any that are the same, highlight these. If any items are not on your list but are on your mate's, and you would be willing to try them, put an X next to them. Then make a plan together to invest time in the highlighted activities and consider how you might also prioritize the items with an X.

4. *Laughing together*: to increase the laughter quotient in your marriage, here are a few ideas:

a. Get silly. Let yourself be playful!

b. Watch a television show or movie that makes you both laugh.

c. Find a funny YouTube video or an app and send it to your spouse during the workday. Monk-e-maker is especially funny, as you can send your spouse a picture of themselves mocked up to look like a monkey.

d. Set up some funny notifications that will pop up on your mate's phone.

e. Develop an inside joke.

f. Find at least three things that are guaranteed to make you both laugh and do them regularly!

5. *Physical touch*: sit down together and write out the top five ways you each like to receive touch. Perhaps you enjoy a warm hug, holding hands, or a back rub. Maybe what feels good to your mate is an arm around their waist, a

foot massage, or sitting cuddled on the sofa. Write out your preferences and share them with one another. Then commit yourself to offering your mate one item on their list each day.

6. *Compromise*: pick an issue that has been a source of disagreement upon which you can compromise.

   a. Take time, individually, to write your position on the issue briefly. Include the reasons you believe your position to be reasonable.

   b. Ask yourself if there is anything from your family history that might be influencing your position. (Usually, the more intensely you feel about the issue, the more likely there is an important history to it.) This will give you some clues about why your position seems so right to you.

   c. Ask yourself: If you didn't get your way, what are the feelings that would come up for you? What are your concerns as to what might happen? What might that lead to? What would your feelings be then?

   d. Before you meet with your mate, ask yourself if you feel ready to be openhearted about finding a solution together. If not, you may have some protectors you need to calm before trying to work it out. Once you feel calm inside, meet with your mate and share the feelings you discovered that came up around the issue.

   e. Invite your mate to brainstorm possible solutions that would take into consideration both of your feelings.

      1) Decide what is nonnegotiable (i.e., we are getting married, both families need to be fairly represented, it can't cost over $30K) and what is negotiable (i.e., the pricey vendor for the cake, paying for Uncle Johnny's flight, inviting all "second-tier" relatives).

      2) Brainstorm as many solutions to these as possible without evaluating. Write them down.

3) Go back over this list and consider the pros and cons of each. Make a check mark by those that are most feasible.

4) Together, decide on one solution, knowing none are perfect.

5) In two weeks, evaluate your compromise and decide if it's working or if you want to revisit the list and select another solution.

f. Express appreciation to your mate for their willingness to understand your feelings and move toward compromise.

9

Initiate Intimacy

Fear is the great enemy of intimacy. Fear makes us run away from each other or cling to each other but does not create true intimacy.

Henri Nouwen

What does intimacy mean to you? Free-flowing conversation? A deep sense of trust? Warm affection? Sexual connection? Intimacy may include all of these. But at its core, intimacy means being deeply known and loved as well as deeply knowing and loving the other. Real intimacy makes us feel alive because someone has taken great care to look into the depths of our soul and see us for who we truly are.

Remember our castle imagery? Each of us is a castle with a moat and drawbridge. When we feel another is safe and desirable, we lower our drawbridge over the moat and invite that person to enter. Once inside, they can see the vulnerabilities of the castle. Where there is love, every room and garden in the castle may be freely explored and the vulnerabilities are protected by the lover. Such intimate exploration involves each of you being open and transparent with your emotions, your bodies, and your spiritual selves.

For some, the word *intimacy* has scary connotations. In letting someone into our castles, we risk being rejected or re-wounded. We may fear the other person might not be trustworthy and could use their access to exploit us. Intimacy can also trigger feelings that we're "not enough."

Many men fear they can't meet their wives' need for emotional intimacy. Women frequently report they cannot keep up with their husbands' desire for sexual intimacy. The word *intimacy* itself stirs up feelings of inadequacy and defensiveness. Although marriage was meant to provide our deepest need for companionship and completeness, it can become a place of expectation, performance pressure, and guardedness.

Our pictures of intimacy can also be tainted by what we see in the media. Most often sex is portrayed as hot, steamy, and self-gratifying, giving couples a self-focused picture of the way sex should be in their marriage.

> Although marriage was meant to provide our deepest need for companionship and completeness, it can become a place of expectation, performance pressure, and guardedness.

You're likely aware of popular television shows like *The Bachelor*, in which a man selects a wife from a pool of women whom he dates and interviews. Eventually he narrows the group down to finalists with whom he has a night of sex in the "fantasy suite" before he makes his final decision.

If you stepped back and asked what images of "intimacy" are represented, you could deduce that intimacy is about the chemistry of attraction, a hot sexual encounter, and superficial conversation. But true intimacy is profoundly different.

A thriving, lifelong marriage is experienced through the emotional intimacy of best friends, the sexual intimacy of lovers, and the spiritual intimacy of two becoming one. True intimacy involves a willingness to be totally open with one another in these three key areas.

Because intimacy requires such openness, it begins with knowing yourself. To allow someone into your fears, desires, hopes and dreams, and strengths and weaknesses, you need to have clarity about what those are. Being truly intimate starts with being connected to your own heart.

Intimacy happens over time. Since being open and vulnerable requires that you feel safe, revealing your heart and true self can occur only as your trust in the other person grows. As you learn that they are willing to guard your confidences, seek your well-being, and be gracious with your weaknesses and faults, you share more and more of yourself with them. As you risk exposing your most vulnerable feelings and thoughts, and find your mate holds them as precious treasures, the safety in your relationship develops.

Emotional Intimacy

Emotional intimacy is the capacity to share your deepest feelings with your mate and receive theirs with understanding and empathy. It involves creating a safe haven where each of you can feel fully comfortable revealing your true selves.

Fear is the greatest hindrance to emotional intimacy. If we hide our authentic selves, fearing rejection or hurt, we can't enjoy deep emotional connection with our mate. If we anxiously cling to our spouse due to our own insecurities, they will not feel free to be themselves—a necessary condition for true closeness. If we become demanding out of a fear that we won't get our needs met, we sabotage the very connection we desire.

Being intimate is a choice. It requires risk. Exposing the deepest parts of yourself to your partner can be uncomfortable. It may seem safer to remain behind the barriers of protection that shield you from potentially being rejected.

However, if you want to be known and loved, you must let down your drawbridge. Being intimate with someone is always proactive. It involves initiating. You choose to reveal or hide yourself. Your mate can enter your castle by invitation only.

When a wife invites her husband into the tender parts of herself, and he is attentive, interested, and kind, she feels valued and loved and opens herself more to him. When he realizes he doesn't need to solve anything for her, or persuade her to think differently, he can simply listen and try to understand, which will result in her feeling deep affection for him.

If her vulnerability is met with impatience, indifference, or discomfort, the wife will shut her feelings away and insert one more brick into the barrier. Many husbands struggle to understand that what their wives need is simple. Just being there with her, giving her his full attention, is all she usually needs. No solutions. No battle plans. Just being there.

When a husband invites his wife into his vulnerable feelings and she is loving, respectful, and generous in response, he feels a warm connection to her. Because respect is so critical for men, revealing what he may consider to be weakness is especially difficult. A savvy wife realizes this and is very affirming of his strengths as she listens attentively.

If, however, she is critical or gives advice, he will likely shut down. Most wives don't understand that their husbands deeply long for them to believe in them. A wife's efforts to improve her husband, or tell him what he should do, sound like disbelief and thus cause him to withdraw.

Both husband and wife have a role in creating safety and intimacy in their relationship.

Some people believe they aren't very good at sharing their thoughts and emotions. You may have grown up in an environment where feelings were minimized or, even worse, criticized. You may have learned early to hide yourself and only put forward what your parents allowed or could tolerate.

Ask yourself, *What scares me about being fully vulnerable with my mate? What do I withhold? What do I fear?* Giving yourself permission to feel and to give expression to what you feel may be difficult at first. As with any new skill, with practice you will become more able to identify your feelings and reveal them.

Ask your mate, "What can I do or say (or *not* do or say) that will help you feel more comfortable and safe in sharing yourself with me?" Try to listen non-defensively and take their feedback to heart.

You may wonder, *Why bother? Why go to all this work if it feels so uncomfortable?* The answer is simple. You are wired for intimate relationship. The Bible says that God designed you with a yearning to be known and loved, to have someone see you and love you for who you really are.[1] He designed you primarily for relationship with himself. Because he made you, he knows and loves you more intimately than any human possibly could.

But he also designed you for intimate relationship with another person.[2] A beautiful picture of intimacy is provided in the biblical account of Adam and Eve. Prior to the creation of Eve, Adam was alone. To provide for Adam's deepest needs for relationship, God made Eve and presented her to Adam. Adam instantly recognized her as his counterpart. He was captivated.

The account then goes on to say that they were both "naked, and they felt no shame."[3] They felt no fear of vulnerability, no need to hide their bodies or their hearts. They could be fully known and fully loved. There were no hindrances, wounds, or preconceived notions from the media or elsewhere that would distort their vision of their mate's intrinsic created beauty or their value as an equal partner in the dance of life. They received one another as pure gift. It is a beautiful picture of emotional, physical, and spiritual intimacy. This is what we were made to enjoy.

This total picture is often lost today. Men will associate intimacy with sex, women with emotional connection. Real intimate encounter includes both. The key to becoming intimate companions is to create a safe place where you can be free to share your deepest thoughts and feelings and enjoy the pleasure of unrestrained sexual closeness.

Sexual Intimacy

Sex is the most vulnerable and intimate expression of giving ourselves freely to each other as husband and wife in marriage. God created it as a gift through which spouses give and receive pleasure and experience nurture and a deep sense of belonging. Sex bonds us like no other experience in life.

The key to becoming intimate companions is to create a safe place where you can be free to share your deepest thoughts and feelings and enjoy the pleasure of unrestrained sexual closeness.

God gave us our sexual organs for a reason—more than one, actually. For reproduction, to be sure. But clearly he also wanted us to enjoy our spouse's body. Just look at the physiological evidence. Due to their larger pre-optic area of the hypothalamus, men have an inclination to be visually stimulated and respond to a woman's body when they see one. Men also produce ten times more testosterone than women do, which accounts for the fact that men tend to think about sex far more often than their wives.

Women are endowed with a clitoris, which has only one function: sexual pleasure. Cultures that have a distorted view of male/female sexuality sometimes remove part or all of this organ to prevent female sexual excitement. They are violating the divine design. God gave women a clitoris because he clearly wants wives to enjoy the sexual experience every bit as much as their husbands do. Women, also, have much higher levels of estrogen than men, which promotes female sexual behavior.

When women give birth, their bodies surge with oxytocin, which allows them to relax so their milk flows and heightens their sense of love and attachment to their babies. Oxytocin is sometimes referred to as the "bonding hormone," in that it creates a sense of trust and attachment.[4] The hormone is calming, reduces stress, and promotes a sense of safety. Dr. Louann Brizendine, in *The Female Brain*, reports that "oxytocin is naturally released in the brain after a twenty-second hug from a partner—sealing the bond between the huggers and triggering the brain's trust circuits."[5]

When husbands and wives are in the throes of passion, oxytocin surges to five times[6] its normal level in both partners, allowing them to feel relaxed, content, and deeply bonded.[7] Additionally, orgasm triggers another neuro-hormone, vasopressin, which interacts with a man's testosterone, boosting his energy, attention, and aggression. It causes him to be intently focused on his partner even when she is not present and stimulates monogamous behavior and parental nurture.[8] It would appear we have hormonal motivation to stay emotionally and sexually connected to our mate!

These physical realities reveal that we were made to enjoy our spouse physically. Men and women experience their sex drive differently but both are created to enjoy sexual pleasure and fulfillment.[9] Clifford and Joyce Penner note, "Each New Testament passage that addresses the husband-wife sexual relationship either begins or ends with a command for mutuality."[10]

But our culture has focused so much on male pleasure and female acquiescence that we have lost sight of God's original intent. The beautiful mutuality we were made for has been buried by distortions, resentments, demands, and expectations that have robbed our physical connection.

Because our sexual relationship is the place where we experience our most intimate oneness and vulnerability, it can also be the place of our deepest hurt.

Broken Sexuality

Our sexuality has suffered from two debilitating extremes—the seeking of personal gratification in sexual encounter and the denial of the importance and beauty of the sexual relationship. These two extremes can create a cycle of sexual dysfunction that damages many marriages.

Ryan and Sarah had become caught in a devitalizing pattern. After the birth of their first child six years ago, Ryan became frustrated with the infrequency of sexual connection. He felt rejected when he initiated sex with Sarah and she put him off or dismissed his overtures.

Having been exposed to pornography as a teen, he started viewing it as a way to satisfy his desire for excitement and stimulation. In the years that followed, Ryan engaged in porn whenever he felt stressed or distant from Sarah. Sarah was unaware of this habit, although she noticed Ryan was becoming more aloof and staying up late many nights. The issue exploded when their six-year-old daughter saw Dad's computer one night on the way to the bathroom.

When they entered my office on a cold January day, both were distressed. Ryan's face was flushed and defiant. He was obviously not happy to be there. Sarah sat in the chair opposite, bent over with her face in her hands, as she told me about the incident with their six-year-old.

"He just doesn't care that he's damaging our daughter," Sarah said, struggling to hold back tears. "All he cares about is himself!"

"You are so overreacting!" Ryan blurted out. "You think Maddy is going to be scarred for life over one picture that was on the screen for a split second?!"

"What she has," Sarah countered, "is a picture of her dad looking at the image of a naked woman. How do you think that makes her feel about you? Or herself?"

"You are blowing this so out of proportion."

I needed to intercept this cycle of attack and defensiveness. "Let's slow this down a bit so we can understand what's really going on here. Sarah, how did you find out about what Maddy saw?"

"The next morning, she came down for breakfast and was unusually quiet. I asked her if anything was wrong, and she told me that she had seen a picture on Daddy's computer that bothered her. When I asked what it was, she told me it was a naked woman. I just about hit the roof, but I knew I had to stay calm for her. I asked her if she saw anything else. She said no. But she said that Daddy told her it was 'no big deal,' that he was just surfing the internet for our next vacation. That was a lie!"

"What were you feeling inside when you first heard this from Maddy?"

"I was angry," Sarah said. "He didn't protect our daughter."

"Any other feelings?" I prompted.

"I felt hurt and betrayed."

"And what did you do or say?"

"I called Ryan at work and told him what Maddy said. I told him we needed to talk when he got home. Then I hung up."

I turned to Ryan. "When she called you, what went on inside you?"

"I was embarrassed and angry. My coworkers could hear her ranting," Ryan said.

"Did you feel anything else?"

"I was worried that Maddy was disturbed. And defensive because Sarah was yelling and I felt attacked."

As we discussed the situation further, I learned that when Ryan got home, he yelled at Sarah for embarrassing him at work. She accused him of caring more about his reputation than his family. Both resorted to name-calling and contempt. As we were able to slow the reactivity and identify the feelings that were underlying it, each became aware of their internal fears and protectors.

Ryan admitted that he had viewed pornography "occasionally" over the years, stating that it was "normal" and that "all guys do it." He had reasoned that, since Sarah didn't know, it wasn't really hurting their marriage. Viewing pornography made him feel more alive, but afterward he felt ashamed.

Sarah expressed the hurt and insecurity she felt as Ryan turned to pornography to meet his sexual desires. Her father had had a brief affair during her parents' marriage, and she still carried the pain of that betrayal and its ensuing havoc on the family. She had vowed to never tolerate any infidelity in her marriage.

She also admitted that her attitude toward sex had been dismissive and that Ryan's initiation had become a bother to her. She had rationalized that, as she was the mom of two active kids, Ryan should understand her level of exhaustion and not add to her plate by expressing a desire for sex. Over time, she had become critical of his frequent sexual desires.

My first order of business was to educate this couple regarding pornography and sexual addiction. I explained that dopamine, a neurotransmitter, is a key component in the reward/motivation pathways in the brain. The body releases dopamine in response to any activity that produces pleasure or promotes life (such as eating, planting a garden, sex, or pornography).

As Norman Doidge clarifies in his book *The Brain That Changes Itself*:

> The reward center uses two different pleasure systems, one that excites and another that satisfies. The first system motivates us to go after things; it is largely fueled by dopamine. The second system makes us feel satisfied and happy after accomplishing something. It's run by endorphins. Porn activates both of the reward center's pleasure systems, but the wanting system is stronger than the satisfying system; porn hyper-activates our wanting system, pumping out dopamine in response to each new image. As a result, the user can get caught in a loop of wanting, using, pumping out a bunch of dopamine, in response to new images found while using, and then wanting even more.[11]

Essentially, dopamine can hook a man's brain on porn. The more he views, the weaker the brain pathway to the normal arousal experiences of touch, cuddling, and the visual stimulation of looking at his real partner becomes. Porn creates a new pathway, which requires ever more stimulating images to return the user to the same level of pleasure.

Pornography can become a stubborn habit and, in some cases, build into a full-blown addiction. Many porn users report not being able to be aroused by anything but porn. They find that they need to look at porn more often or find more hard-core versions to get the same effect.[12]

Regardless of whether the partner knows, porn damages the marriage relationship. It warps the user's idea of what sex is, creates secrecy, and breaks trust. Additionally, viewing porn can impact what the user expects of his partner.

> When a person uses porn, their brain is wiring together what they're seeing in porn with the feelings of arousal it creates, building new brain maps for both what they think is sexy and what they expect from their partner.[13]

Many partners feel inadequate because they are unable to compete with the pornography. Not only do they feel betrayed but, in many cases, partners exhibit symptoms of trauma.[14]

Even in the most mainstream porn, the sexual acts shown are degrading toward women and focused on male pleasure. This kind of sex is worlds apart from the mutually pleasurable, mutually honoring sexual intimacy characteristic of healthy marriages.

If you or your mate is involved in pornography, there is help. A good book to begin with is *Healing the Wounds of Sexual Addiction* by Mark Laaser.[15] Two websites that may be helpful are www.fightthenewdrug.org and www.pureintimacy.org. I recommended to Ryan that he get professional help and suggested that he go to www.iitap.com to find a certified sex-addiction therapist.

Next I helped Ryan and Sarah understand each other's deep needs and emotions. Sarah had a strong desire to be Ryan's one and only love interest. Ryan was surprised that his viewing of pornography made Sarah feel very insecure about her body. Helping him understand the pressure women have in our culture to have the perfect body enabled him to see how his behavior had been, to her, like throwing salt in a wound.

Ryan also admitted that his libido for sex with Sarah had diminished the more frequently he had masturbated with the pornography. He was able to see how his dishonesty affected the relationship as it created a wedge in their ability to be open and intimate. Although he felt helpless to draw Sarah into more sexual engagement, he saw how he had violated the relationship by seeking sexual satisfaction elsewhere.

Sarah was able to see how her disinterest in sex was damaging the relationship. Early beliefs about sex had hindered her from full engagement with Ryan. Attitudes like "all guys ever want is sex" or "sex is all about him" permeated her thinking. Although she and her husband had enjoyed frequent sexual connection early in their marriage, once Maddy was born Sarah had started channeling her energies to her role as a mom. When Ryan pursued her for sexual connection, she tried to ignore him or accused him of being selfish and obsessed.

In time, Sarah realized how her early beliefs had robbed her of enjoyment of her own sexual pleasure. She had been so focused on Ryan's satisfaction that she hadn't learned how to guide her husband toward her erogenous zones. Both she and Ryan had bought into the "sex is for the guy" mentality, which caused Ryan to have a predatory mentality and Sarah to withhold. Both attitudes had robbed them of the joy of mutual pleasuring.

After a few sessions, Ryan acknowledged that his use of porn was hurting his marriage. He expressed sincere remorse and began to work on rebuilding trust. Sarah acknowledged that her dismissiveness was wounding a core part of her husband. Although

Ryan's interest had been hijacked by pornography, seeing her role in their dysfunction gave Sarah motivation to help repair their sexual relationship.

The Impact of Shame and Abuse

Because our sexual selves are so vulnerable to wounding, the experience of shame in this area of our lives is not uncommon. Many women feel insecure about their bodies. Comparing themselves to other women, such as models on magazine covers or actresses, they come to believe the body they've been given is "not enough."

If a woman has been abused, molested, or raped, she may conclude that she is damaged or bad. In his book *The Wounded Heart*, Dan Allender describes the impact of shame and the dread of rejection that abused women experience: "It is the terror that if our dark soul is discovered, we will never be enjoyed, nor desired, nor pursued by anyone."[16] Men who have been sexually abused can also suffer from profound feelings of shame.

Because sex is one of the most beautiful expressions of intimate love, it is also very vulnerable to distortions and misuse. If you have been sexually violated, you know the wound of having this tender part of you abused for someone's pleasure. You may even have come to a place of despising your own body because of the pain it represents. To you I would offer a word of encouragement: your body is beautiful, and just because someone else used it for their own purposes doesn't make it any less beautiful. God made you and loves you, and he desires to make something beautiful from the ashes of your abuse.[17]

You may even have come to associate sex with perversion, bad memories, or pain. If so, I encourage you to seek the help of a qualified therapist who can help you overcome the traumatic injury you have experienced and restore your ability to enjoy the gift of physical closeness with your spouse.

Although God wants to restore all of our areas of brokenness, I think he may have a special heart for healing our sexual intimacy, because it touches our deepest vulnerability and provides our deepest human connection. It was his very first gift to us as male and female. He desires that we enjoy this gift to the fullest.[18]

For Wives Only

Ladies, I'd like to talk with you for a moment about how you are made physically. Guys, if you're reading this, let me provide a word of caution: resist the urge to become your wife's self-appointed sex coach. Let her be in charge of her own learning and invite you into the process when she's ready. If you just want to find her "hot buttons" so you can more quickly get her to intercourse and your own sexual pleasure, you will lose the opportunity of becoming a savvy sexual partner. Your wife needs time to explore her body. If you seize control she will not feel safe and will likely pull back.

We women are more sexually complex than our husbands. Most of a man's nerve cells are located in one organ. But women have multiple erogenous zones, which respond differently on different days.

So wives, get to know yourselves and what brings you physical pleasure. You may need to get some books to help you explore this part of yourself, such as *The Good Girl's Guide to Great Sex* by Sheila Gregoire or *The Gift of Sex* by Clifford and Joyce Penner. Knowing about your body is a crucial part of learning about your individual preferences.

About half of all women sometimes experience orgasm through intercourse. Only 25 percent are consistently orgasmic during intercourse and 20 percent seldom or never have an orgasm during intercourse.[19] Approximately 70 percent of women require clitoral stimulation for orgasm.[20] It is safe to say that intercourse is not the primary key to sexual satisfaction for most women.

During intercourse, the clitoris is indirectly stimulated but may need more direct stimulation for orgasm to occur. Some women are more vaginally sensitive due primarily to two parts of their anatomy: the pubococcygeus (PC) muscle which surrounds and controls the lower third of the wall of the vaginal barrel, and the Grafenberg or G-spot, a mass of tissue located on the front wall of the vagina just beyond the PC muscle, which enlarges during sexual stimulation. These areas can be wonderful sources of sexual stimulation.

When you pay attention to and pursue what is pleasurable to you, you will be more interested in sexual engagement and more satisfied afterward. Your husband has no way of knowing what is going on in your body. Communicating with him your unique sensitivities and preferences from moment to moment is beneficial to a full and satisfying sex life.

Here are some suggestions for enjoying sexual intimacy with your husband:

1. *Mentally shift into sexual gear.* A woman's most important sexual organ is her mind. Sex is a decision you make mentally. Women are great at multitasking. Our minds can often wander during sex. It is important to accept that reality but turn our attention back to our bodies and what they are feeling and enjoying, even as other thoughts will pass through our minds.

   Have you been viewing your husband's sexual drive as a nuisance? Have you slipped into an attitude of obligation? Have you allowed other responsibilities and interests to crowd out your energy for lovemaking? Your mind may need renewing in this area. As Sheila Gregoire states in her book on sex for young wives, "The key to a man's heart isn't to placate him; it's to actually engage in the process."[21]

   If you have no energy or desire for sex, you might simply need more rest and self-care. But you may also have some negative messages that are preventing you from enjoying this aspect of your married life. If so, therapy could be beneficial in helping you reclaim your interest and joy in this area.

Here are some ways to get your mind engaged:

a. Plan a romantic or playful sexual encounter. The planning will get you focused and energized.

b. Set boundaries with whatever deprives you and your husband of intimate moments together (e.g., demands of children, distraction of television, an unlocked door).

c. Train your mind to "think sex." After an exhausting day taking care of the kids or working, the last thing on your mind is sex. You're preoccupied with what still needs to get done. But intimate physical closeness with your husband is as important as many of those tasks, if not more so. Take a few moments to consider when would be a good time to initiate sex—such as when your kiddos are asleep or your work requirements are the lightest. Schedule it on the calendar and protect that time from intrusions.

2. *Nurture your sexual feelings.* Learn about the parts of your anatomy that are most sensitive to sexual pleasure. Also pay attention to when during the month or day you are most sexually interested or responsive (e.g., at ovulation, in the morning).

Know your optimal conditions. Are you more sexually responsive after a time of playfulness? During a candlelight dinner? Following an extended time of talking or holding? And know what stimulates you: a romantic comedy, verbal affirmation, his undressing you, or passionate expressions of affection?

Exercise your body. Energy is essential to feeling sexual. A good jog or even just a few minutes at the gym may increase your natural hormone levels, fueling your desire.

Invite your husband to help you relax. Is there something he can take off your plate to allow you to be more available?

3. *Know your husband.* Ask your husband what he finds most pleasurable in your lovemaking. For a man, physical intimacy often opens the door to emotional closeness.

Intimacy for men is also about companionship. He wants to enjoy adventures in and outside of bed. He doesn't want you to merely capitulate in sex to meet his needs, although he might settle for that if it's all he thinks he can hope for. He wants to be partners in a mutual experience. Join him in the adventure.

Going after your own pleasure isn't selfish. On the contrary, it's a turn-on. Your husband wants to satisfy you sexually. Work on your self-consciousness and inhibitions so you can become more daring in your love life. Your husband is hard-wired to be visually stimulated, and he enjoys the beauty of your body. Although you may think your body needs improvement in one or more areas, he is more easily satisfied. Allow him to see you naked.

Let these words from an Anglican wedding ceremony inspire you:

With my body I will adore you.
And your body alone will I cherish.
I will with my body declare your worth.[22]

4. *Accept pleasure and give it.* We are often more comfortable giving than receiving. Give yourself permission to take in compliments and physical pleasure and to receive stimulation.

For Husbands Only

As men, you naturally have a goal-oriented, competitive approach to life. Much of your work life has been focused on getting results. But that mindset will not lead to deep love, passion, or intimacy with your wife. "Sex is not about conquering, achieving or scoring; sex is about relating."[23]

Being a great lover involves some critical shifts in the way you think about and approach sex. You need to change your perspective from pursuing an objective to enjoying the process of lovemaking. Your wife's more complicated sexual makeup and multiple erogenous zones require you to take on the role of a symphony conductor, exploring nuances and inviting discovery. If you believe you have to be the quarterback with the winning pass, you might end up with a frustrating loss.

Be receptive to learning about your wife's body and her desires. Keep in mind that what feels good to her changes with every encounter. You'll need to be attentive and responsive to what brings her pleasure in any given moment.

If you think you've found the right button to turn her on every time, you will become frustrated and impatient when that technique doesn't stimulate the same response consistently. Becoming a savvy lover is like being a surfer—you have to be tuned in to the waves and allow them to guide your next move in order to have the ride of your life and not wipe out.

Here are some tips to help you become a great lover:

1. *Serve your way to better sex*. Because you are more visually stimulated than your wife, and can reach an orgasm far more quickly, seek to serve her first. Women typically take three to ten times longer to reach orgasm than the average man.[24] That's likely because her brain's anxiety center, the amygdala, needs to shut down to make her available for the experience. As Louann Brizendine explains:

Female sexual turn-on begins, ironically, with a brain turn-off. The impulses can rush to the pleasure centers and trigger an orgasm only if the amygdala—the fear and anxiety center of the brain—has been deactivated. Before the amygdala has been turned off, any last-minute worry—about work, about the kids, about schedules, about getting dinner on the table—can interrupt the march toward orgasm.[25]

So, slow down and enjoy the process of lovemaking. Focus on her enjoyment rather than your climax. Listen carefully to her verbal and nonverbal communication. She will sense your patience and selfless interest, and that will be a turn-on for her!

2. *Bring back romance.* When you first fell in love with your wife, how did you communicate your feelings? Did you call her frequently? Leave her cards, notes, little signs she was on your mind? Invest time in creating special moments and memories? Were you tender and patient? Resume those behaviors that made her fall in love with you. Let her know you are captivated by her.

Be intentional about the atmosphere and environment surrounding your relationship. How you treated her that day, whether or not you responded to her needs, if your tone was harsh or tender—all these factor into whether she feels ready to give herself to you physically.

3. *Offer to help.* Be conscious of all the roles and responsibilities your wife has to balance. When a woman has children to care for, a home to manage, extended family concerns, work, or projects she's involved in, it's easy to feel overwhelmed.

Find ways to lighten her load and let her know you appreciate all that she has to handle. For example, if your wife is a stay-at-home mom and you work outside the home, you may think she should be able to easily handle everything. But even if she had limitless capability and energy, she doesn't want to feel alone in her load. To your wife, your interest in helping her is sexy. Sex begins in the kitchen . . . by you helping with the dishes!

4. *Listen well.* Women verbally process in a nonlinear, free-flowing way. Thinking out loud helps her connect emotions and thoughts. Your willingness to listen without giving advice or trying to fix everything is a gift and an expression of your love for her. It is also something she will deeply appreciate and respond to. Feeling more emotionally connected to you makes her more available for physical connection.

If you listen well, you will discover some keys to your wife's heart and her desire to connect with you physically. What conditions cause her to be most sexually interested? After a time of playfulness? When you have her favorite shirt on? In the morning, afternoon, or evening? Right after you both shower? As she watches you play with the kids?

What form of non-genital touch does she most appreciate? A hug, holding hands, a foot rub? Treating your sexual relationship as a place of exploration will take the focus off demands and performance and introduce a sense of discovery into your lovemaking.

How you experience your sex drive is very different from your wife. What opens her to sexual intimacy is to feel treasured. Rather than pursuing your wife, assure her of her beauty and value. When you love her selflessly, without demands, her heart is drawn toward you and she becomes more open sexually.

A beautiful example of this dynamic is in the story of Solomon, who delights in his wife and affirms her. His adoration awakens in her a sexual hunger for him: "His mouth is sweetness itself; he is altogether lovely. This is my beloved" (Song of Songs 5:16). Ephesians 5:25 says it another way, "Husbands, go all out in your love for your wives, exactly as Christ did for the church—a love marked by giving, not getting" (MSG).

Sex is a wonderful, bonding aspect of a couple's relationship where they can enjoy a nourishing rhythm of physical connection interspersed with heights of intense passion.

Spiritual Intimacy

Spiritual intimacy is a mutually enjoyed experience of God's presence and involvement in your life as a couple. The Judeo-Christian view of God is that he is personal—he loves us and wants a relationship with each of us.

Think of a braided cord with three strands. If there were only two strands, you might twist the two together as tightly as you could, but once you let go, they would unwind and separate. When you add the third strand and braid the three, a bond is created that holds them all together. Such a cord doesn't unravel easily. As the two of you share hearts that desire to be close to God, a sense of unity and purpose is created that strengthens your marital bond.

Early in our marriage, my husband and I were given the following diagram. Though simple, it has been very helpful for us.

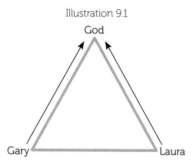

Illustration 9.1

Spiritual intimacy, in the Christian context, is the process of becoming closer to God. As we each grow in our understanding of who God is, and seek to love him and align our lives with his purposes for us, we grow closer to one another. As we trust God more and become more vulnerable with him, we become more vulnerable and open with one another. The primary movement is toward God, and we as a couple benefit from the increased closeness to each other.

Your spiritual intimacy will be enhanced when you learn to pray as a couple. Praying together is a profound experience, as it joins your hearts in the midst of the concerns of your shared life and invites God into the challenges. Praying for your children can help unite you as you ask God for wisdom about each one's unique needs and personality. Acknowledging your shortcomings to God as you pray together can help soften your heart toward each other and enable you to offer forgiveness more quickly. Praying for family members, work pressures, and life's challenges can help you trust God with the realities of your lives and notice together any ways in which you see him at work.

Praying together consistently connects you at a deep level that keeps your relationship focused on what is important. There is no need to impress your spouse with your words as you pray. Keep it simple and sincere.

You may also find it helpful to read a spiritually enriching book or couples devotional together. *Devotions for a Sacred Marriage* by Gary Thomas or *The One Year Love Language Minute Devotional* by Gary Chapman may provide inspiration for your marriage.[26] Tim Keller's *The Meaning of Marriage* is another excellent resource for understanding Christian marriage.[27] You could also read the Bible together. The book of John is a good place to start.

To further grow in your relationship with God and your spouse, find others who are seeking to grow in the same way. You may have been disappointed in organized churches, but finding a Christian community that stimulates you to grow and provides an environment where you can learn and pray with others will be a valuable support to your marriage and your faith.

You may also benefit from the opportunity to serve together—caring for the poor, volunteering, or offering your talents to support the community of faith. Serving side by side allows you to see your spouse's heart in action and will strengthen your marriage bond.

Growing in your spiritual intimacy has incredible benefits for your emotional and sexual intimacy. As you become more confident that God loves you and is trustworthy, you will be able to move toward your mate with more vulnerability and less self-protection. As you spend more time with him, his character will rub off on you. You may become more compassionate, kind, and generous and better able to love your mate without demands or conditions.

By trusting God's good intentions for your marriage, you will become more receptive to your mate, acknowledging that they are in the process of becoming who God designed them to be. You might even see your role in their transformation more clearly.

Though you know your mate has different emotional and sexual needs than you do, and you may already understand how to meet them, your intimacy with God will give you the heart to do so.

If your mate doesn't share your interest in spiritual intimacy, you can still pursue your spiritual growth and allow God's love to permeate your marriage through you.

■ ■ ■

Marriage provides us an enduring context in which to love, to be vulnerable and transparent, and to become intimate companions. Here you can create a safe place where you are free to share your deepest thoughts and feelings, enjoy the pleasure of unrestrained sexual closeness, and nurture your spiritual lives. As you initiate intimacy with your mate and open yourselves to the gift of each other, you will be well on your way to the thriving, lifelong marriage you desire.

Discussion Questions: Chapter 9

Group Questions

1. What does the word *intimacy* mean to you? Do you find yourself more comfortable with one form of intimacy than another (emotional, physical, spiritual, etc.)? What is your picture of what it means to have a truly intimate relationship? Share it with the group.

2. Do you agree that fear is the greatest hindrance to intimacy? Why or why not?

3. Generally speaking, what do you think is a woman's greatest challenge with regard to physical intimacy? What is a husband's greatest challenge? What does Genesis 2:22–25 say about the intimacy God intends for husband and wife?

4. Read Song of Songs 4:16–6:3 and 1 Corinthians 7:3–5. From these verses, do you think God intended for the sexual relationship between a husband and wife to be mutually fulfilling?

5. Read John 17:20–26. In Jesus's prayer for us, what does it say about the intimacy we can enjoy with him and with God?

6. Do you seek a spiritually intimate relationship? Read Ephesians 5:25–32. How is the relationship between husband and wife to be like the relationship between Christ and the church? How could a husband's sacrificial love for his wife and a wife's respect for her husband lead to deepened spiritual intimacy? Share any "best practices" that help your relationship when it comes to spiritual intimacy.

For Personal Reflection

1. The greatest hindrance to intimacy is fear. Important questions you may ask yourself are, *What scares me about being fully vulnerable with my mate? What do I withhold? What do I fear?*

2. What feelings do you have about your sexual relationship with your mate? How would you like it to be different? What would you need to do to move in a more positive direction?

   Of the suggestions mentioned in the "For Wives Only" or "For Husbands Only" sections, is there one thing you would be willing to work on to improve your physical relationship?

3. Have there been any ways you have been robbed (negative sexual messages, sexual abuse) or hijacked (pornography)

that currently hinder the joy of your sexual relationship with your spouse? Are you willing to work on those to bring healing to your marriage? If so, tell your spouse. Resources were provided in the chapter for treating porn abuse and sexual addiction. The help of a qualified therapist can also be a necessary resource for overcoming the impact of sexual abuse and negative messaging about sex.

4. Is becoming spiritually connected important to you? What is your picture as to how that could benefit you and your relationship? If you are interested, see question 4 below for an idea as to how to begin.

Couple Questions

1. What does "emotional intimacy" mean to you? Share with your mate the times in your married life you have felt the closest. What were the factors that caused you to feel so close?

2. Do you feel you can be completely yourself with your mate, including your fears, weaknesses, dreams, and so forth? What hinders such openness between you? What is one thing each of you can do to remove the barrier to a closer relationship? A question you can ask your mate is, "What can I do or say (or *not* do or say) that will help you feel more comfortable and safe in sharing yourself with me?" Try to listen non-defensively and take their feedback to heart.

3. Having read your respective sections on physical intimacy ("For Wives Only" or "For Husbands Only"), share with your mate one thing you are going to work on to improve your physical relationship. Or, if you would like a more specific suggestion regarding improving your sexual life:

   • For wives: thank your husband for his desire to connect with you sexually. Let him know how you feel when you are overwhelmed with tasks and share two things that would help you be more available when he wants to enjoy sex.

- For husbands: thank your wife for all she does to care for you and the family. If she is consistently unavailable sexually, let her know how it feels to you. (She needs to be allowed to say "no" at times.) Be vulnerable. She can't know how you uniquely experience this as a man. Ask her what you can do to help lift her load.

4. If you have an interest in growing your spiritual intimacy, a simple way to do so is to go to www.marriageprayers.today and together pray the simple daily prayer for couples. Some couples enjoy starting their day with the prayer. Others like to do so as they head to bed at night. Whatever your rhythm, it is easy to understand and helps you connect in this heart-to-heart way.

PART 3

Re-visioning Marriage— Changing the Way You Love

10

The Power of a Promise

One advantage of marriage is that, when you fall out of love with him or he falls out of love with you, it keeps you together until you fall back in love again.

Judith Viorst

If you intend to enjoy lasting love—a marriage that withstands the test of time—what can you anticipate will change and what can you trust to remain the same? In the first three chapters of this book we looked at reimagining your marriage, exploring why marriage is such hard work, why it's worth the effort, and cultural trends that warrant some reflection. We also discussed new ways of thinking about your relationship. In the next six chapters we looked at specific ways you can revitalize your marriage by changing the ways you and your spouse relate to each other. In these last chapters, we will explore how to make love last by casting a new vision for your marriage. This new vision is built on the foundation of your promise to each other, which creates the impetus for the new possibilities of your relationship. What can your marriage become?

When a cocoon turns into a butterfly, some parts of the caterpillar remain the same while most parts are transformed into a completely new creature. The parts that stay the same, the imaginal cells, are critical to the process of transformation into the new state. The metamorphosis of marriage is like that. Some parts remain constant while other parts enter the process of becoming something new.

The Contingent Marriage

My husband and I recently bought a house. The paperwork nearly buried us. I had forgotten how much there is to sign and the time it takes to read the fine print. Perhaps the most nail-biting moment in our transaction was the removal of contingencies. In a market where there are lots of buyers, sellers give priority to buyers who have no contingencies. They want to know there's no way the buyer can back out.

Removing all the "ifs" sealed the deal. We now own the house and we haven't looked back. Removing all contingencies in the most important relationship of your life can be nerve-racking as well.

At the urging of my daughter-in-law, I recently watched a television program called *Married at First Sight*. This reality series conducts a social experiment in which three couples meet at the altar without knowing anything about their future spouses—only that they have been matched by a panel of experts.

As I watched this show, I couldn't help but wonder what would attract someone to sign up for this blind commitment. Some of the participants appeared to have long dating histories with no apparent success in finding that special someone. Perhaps giving the "experts" permission to locate their match would take away their guesswork (and, hopefully, their relationship difficulties).

They apparently had more confidence that strangers would be wiser than they would be in making this important life decision. Perhaps they saw their risk as a small investment with potentially high gains, much like a low-cost, high-yield stock, especially since the couples were offered the option of a quick divorce after five weeks if things didn't work out.

What does marriage *mean* to those willing to meet at the altar and potentially divorce five weeks later? What does marriage *mean* to you? Is it a mere contract that can be entered or broken at will? Or is it something greater, something beyond a signed agreement with exit clauses?

The Meaning of Marriage

To some, marriage is an antiquated notion. They view marriage as a piece of paper that is not really necessary if two people love each other, although they may acknowledge it can provide some legal or practical benefits. Others see marriage as a contract between two people to meet each other's needs, live together, and possibly raise a family. In this contemporary view, the relationship is legitimately sustainable only if the needs of each partner are being met. Since the individual's happiness is the primary value, feelings of love and romance are the glue of the contractual relationship. Once the glue loses its stickiness, the contract is no longer deemed binding.

Many marriages operate with such unspoken contingencies. Marriage is seen as a conditional arrangement that protects the rights of both parties in the event one fails to live up to the other's expectations. It focuses attention on what each spouse is or is not contributing to the relationship. It provides an "out" if either partner is perceived as not living up to his or her end of the bargain. The contractual marriage, with its option of "no-fault divorce," allows for dissolution of the marriage if one party isn't feeling love.

Years ago, I attended a wedding that took place in a beautiful outdoor setting with all the family and many friends gathered. The bride was a bit of a free spirit and the groom was a likable, easygoing sort of guy. They looked extremely happy that day, and I thought they would enjoy a long life together. But as they gave each other their vows, they said they were committed "as long as we both shall love."

How long will that last? I wondered. Turns out, after having two sons, they divorced, remarried, and divorced again. True to their vows, their promise stuck as long as they *felt* love and dissolved when the feeling waned.

There have been many times in my years of marriage when I haven't felt love for my husband. There have been plenty of moments when I've been seething mad and seasons when I've felt disconnected. We have a fantastic marriage now. But if we had made feelings of love the criteria for staying together we would have split long ago and missed enjoying the fruit of our labor— and, yes, I mean labor.

Most of us marry with the idea that we are committing to a lifelong relationship. You can't predict the kinds of challenges you will face as you enter marriage. The difficulties are often more than you expected. The realization that you can feel hate for someone you also love can come as a surprise. You can argue passionately over silly little issues as if they were monumental. Your attitude about what marriage is will shape how you navigate those unexpected challenges.

The Power of a Promise

When you state your wedding vows and make a promise to love, honor, and cherish your beloved all the days of your life, you are exercising your freedom in a life-changing way. You are saying that no matter what your history, no matter what your limitations, no matter what the future brings, "I choose you." It is paradoxical in that you are *freely* choosing to *bind yourself* to one person for a lifetime. You are restricting your freedom, forsaking all others, to ensure love. It is the supreme exercise of choice.

The protection provided by promising is captured in a Thornton Wilder play called *The Skin of Our Teeth* when one character tells the other, "I didn't marry you because you were perfect. I didn't even marry you because I loved you. I married you because you gave me a promise. That promise made up for your faults. And the promise I gave you made up for mine. Two imperfect people got married and it was the promise that made the marriage. And when our children were growing up, it wasn't a house that protected them; and it wasn't our love that protected them—it was that promise."[1]

The Judeo-Christian view is that marriage is a promise to love another person unconditionally all the days of your life. There is an old word for this kind of commitment: *covenant*. A covenant is light-years apart from a contractual agreement, as it is far more creative and compelling. Let me explain.

Covenant is a biblical term originally used to describe the nature of God's relationship with the Israel-

When you state your wedding vows and make a promise to love, honor, and cherish your beloved all the days of your life, you are exercising your freedom in a life-changing way. You are saying that no matter what your history, no matter what your limitations, no matter what the future brings, "I choose you."

ites.[2] God had chosen them to be his people and had bound himself to them with irrevocable promises to be with them. It was a unilateral promise that ensured ongoing relationship. The Israelites could mess up—and they did, many times—but God would not abandon them. If they strayed from the covenant, they would not experience the blessings that the secure relationship could provide, but he would not leave them. The relationship was safeguarded.

Although we don't often think of being a parent as having a "covenant" with our children, the way in which we relate to them is very covenantal. We may not like how they behave at any given moment, but we are committed to loving them regardless.

Despite our momentary anger or frustration, we've made an inherent promise to be their parent and be present no matter what happens. It is a one-sided offer that says, "This is how things will always stand between us."[3]

The Bible also speaks of marriage as a covenant. In Malachi 2:14, a man is reminded that his spouse is "your partner, the wife of your marriage covenant." Proverbs 2:17 refers to an unfaithful wife who has "left the partner of her youth and ignored the covenant she made before God." To enter a covenant is to make a one-sided promise to love and be faithful to the other for life. It is unilateral in that you are making a promise *to God* to love your mate, regardless of how they may love or fail to love you.

When you married you likely took vows that promised this kind of constancy. You may have spoken traditional vows, such as, "I take you to be my lawfully wedded husband, and I do promise and covenant, before God and these witnesses, to be your loving and faithful wife. In plenty and in want, in joy and in sorrow, in sickness and in health, as long as we both shall live."

Or perhaps you wrote your own vows. Hopefully you have saved your vows in written form or on a wedding video. Take them out and review them from time to time. They likely included a promise from each of you to love the other for life.

Does the idea of making a covenant promise to love someone without contingencies seem crazy or reckless? To be sure, it is risky. But it is also transformational.

Covenantal marriage changes us. It is to say to our spouse, "I will always be there for you. No matter what happens or what changes, I will be tenacious in how I love you. When you are irritable and frustrated, I will exercise patience. When we fight and argue, I will stretch myself to see your viewpoint and work toward restoring our relationship. I will not expect perfection but will give you room to grow. When my feelings for you have dried up, I will trust that the rains will come and will refresh and renew our love. When we grow distant and life pulls us apart, I will pursue you for connection and work with you to set limits on what causes us to disengage. When we are at odds and I am tempted to look elsewhere for my needs to be met, I will protect myself from seeking love from someone else. I will have eyes only for you. I believe we can work and will give our relationship my all. And when we are thriving and content, I will celebrate our love, marvel at our journey, and continue to invest in strengthening our marriage through all our days ahead."

The marriage covenant is an enduring, total commitment that says, "This is how I will always be toward you." Unlike a contract, it is not conditional or dependent on met expectations or feelings of love. It is within the security of this promise that you can both be freed to truly be yourselves. You create the safety necessary for love to grow. As Daniel Brown points out, "The promises act as benevolent restrictions, eliminating unsettling options. The promise to love does away with the prospect of not loving."[4]

This kind of promise-keeping is powerful. Author Lew Smedes states:

> When you make a promise, you tie yourself to the other person by the unseen fibers of loyalty. You agree to stick with people you are stuck with. When everything else tells them they can count on nothing, they count on you. When they do not have the faintest notion of what in the world is going on around them, they will know that you are going to be there with them. You have created a small sanctuary of trust within the jungle of unpredictability: You have made a promise that you intend to keep.[5]

This sanctuary of trust is imperative for love to grow. When the thrill of infatuation is gone, and you begin to experience real life with a real mate, the covenant you have entered will keep you together while love matures.

With the assurance that your marriage will withstand the tests of time and challenges, you and your spouse are liberated to expose your true selves. And when you bring your true selves to each other, the ground is fertile for growth.

Some have argued that having this certainty would cause couples to take each other for granted. They claim that having some insecurity about the relationship forces both parties to keep their game sharp and put their best foot forward. I have never seen evidence of this. What I do see in couples who are unable to fully commit is a guardedness and self-protection that keep them from being themselves. They hide from each other and focus on what they're not getting from the relationship. They feel unsafe exposing their vulnerabilities because they don't trust their mates to be there for them.

> When the thrill of infatuation is gone, and you begin to experience real life with a real mate, the covenant you have entered will keep you together while love matures.

Viewing marriage as a permanent union has significant benefits. It provides a foundation that allows you to withstand the tremors of disillusioned expectations, conflicting needs, and waning feelings of love. It's like a seismic retrofit on your relationship that helps it withstand all the pulls and shakes of life.

When James and Amy entered therapy, they were caught in the insecure tension of not knowing whether their relationship would last. It was clear to Amy that James was not meeting her needs for time and attention. She was considering a separation as a way of alerting James to the depth of her pain.

James experienced an increasing demand from Amy to be available, which made him feel stifled and inadequate. He, too, was considering leaving to relieve himself of the burden of her emotional needs.

With each being unsure of the commitment of the other, their protectors were working hard to guard their own positions.

During four months of therapy, James became aware of Amy's young part that longed for connection with her father. He realized that his pulling away was activating her fear of not being wanted, not belonging. He also became more conscious of how he had, early in life, cut himself off from his own need for closeness, since such desires were dismissed by his parents.

One afternoon James entered my office with a sense of determination. "I have something I want to say to Amy," he announced.

Amy looked puzzled. "What is it?" she asked, clearly caught off guard.

"I just want you to know, I'm not going anywhere. I am in this for good."

Amy teared up. "What do you mean?"

James took her hand. "When you were talking about your young part last week, and you said she was worried I might leave, it hit me. She needs to know I'm staying."

Tears streamed down Amy's face. "That feels really good." Her shoulders relaxed, as if offloading a heavy burden. She squeezed James's hand. "I want you to know I'm all-in too."

"I'm glad." James smiled. "I love you, Amy, and I'm willing to do whatever it takes to make our marriage work. I know I've got some changing to do. I hope you can be patient."

"Knowing you're open to growing is all I need," Amy said. "I'll try to give you more space."

James and Amy were beginning to reap the rewards of committed love. By taking the prospect of leaving off their plate, they were free to reinvest energy in their growth as a couple. Their openness to self-awareness and compassionate understanding of each other paved the way for the transformation of their marriage they had been seeking.

The promise to stay is like the imaginal cells of the cocoon, so necessary to its metamorphosis into a butterfly. (If you have been thinking about your marriage in a more contractual way, and you would like to re-vision your marriage as a covenant relationship, see appendix C.)

Discussion Questions: Chapter 10

Group and Couple Questions

1. Have you been seeing your marriage as more of a contract or a covenant? Where do you notice any contingencies that have slipped into your thinking about your relationship?

2. "To enter a covenant is to make a one-sided promise to love and be faithful to the other for life. It is unilateral in that you are making a promise *to* God to love your mate regardless of how they love or fail to love you." When you think about making such a unilateral promise, what feelings come up for you? Read Malachi 2:14, Proverbs 2:17, and Matthew 19:3–9. How does a covenant commitment make a difference in how you view marriage?

3. Lew Smedes states,

   > When you make a promise, you tie yourself to the other person by the unseen fibers of loyalty. You agree to stick with people you are stuck with. When everything else tells them they can count on nothing, they count on you. When they do not have the faintest notion of what in the world is going on around them, they will know that you are going to be there with them. You have created a small sanctuary of trust within the jungle of unpredictability: You have made a promise that you intend to keep.[6]

   Have you, at some time in your marriage, experienced that "small sanctuary of trust"? How has your promise made this possible?

4. If you still know or have a copy of your vows, you might want to take some time to share them in your group. Notice together what commitments you made. You might even want to renew your vows (see appendix C) with your group as witnesses.

For Personal Reflection

1. Have you been seeing your marriage as more of a contract or a covenant? Where do you notice any contingencies that have slipped into your thinking about your relationship? How does a covenant commitment make a difference in how you view marriage?

2. Laura states, "With the assurance that your marriage will withstand the tests of time and challenges, you and your spouse are liberated to expose your true selves." How does the knowledge that your mate is committed to you for life allow you to let down your guard and be more fully vulnerable? How does it promote your personal growth? How does the promise you made protect your marriage?

11

Marriage as a Catalyst for Change

If you didn't want to be improved, you shouldn't have gotten married.

Nancy (Mrs. Scott) Stanley

Intimate relationship is powerful. You can choose to be your spouse's biggest fan and closest confidant or their harshest critic. Your relationship has the power to crush you or to re-create you both into more loving human beings. You get to choose which it will be. You can't control your mate but you can control how you choose to respond to them. Your marriage provides you with unparalleled opportunities for personal transformation.

Usually, the impetus for our positive growth is a challenging situation. When we face difficulties we are pulled out of our comfort zone and nudged to dig deep and discover what we're made of. Our image of ourselves as kind, reasonable, and generous is turned on its head as we see the depth of our self-interest. It is in our most intimate relationship that our real selves emerge and we are required to self-examine and adjust. Marriage provides that opportunity. It is the perfect laboratory in which to learn to love well.

It's likely you didn't enter your marriage relationship with a desire to change. Your partner seemed pretty perfect for you, and you felt comfortable with yourself. You enjoyed similar interests and viewpoints, for the most part, and as you looked ahead, life seemed like a smooth road. Some bumps, a few detours, but mostly navigable. Most of us don't expect that the road ahead will involve serious potholes and mountainous climbs.

Change in marriage is a given, because it is the most trying and exposing of all our human relationships.

Most of us didn't consider ourselves selfish until we got married. When our mate's needs confront our own and someone's got to give, we are faced with our own unwillingness to compromise. When our mate desires us to show affection and we don't feel like it, we are pushed outside of our convenience. When we have to consider the well-being of another as we make life decisions, we are stretched to move beyond our self-focused concern with our own priorities.

Not only that, but our mate has a front-row seat to our shortcomings and they're usually all too willing to point them out! When they do, we can either defend ourselves or give our mate's observations serious consideration. We can refuse to change or take a look at ourselves and see what might need some attention. Marriage is like that—it exposes our weaknesses and helps us see ourselves in more detail. We get to choose what we do with the information, but more often than not their input is at least worthy of an honorable mention. We would do well to consider it if we want to become our best selves.

Author Gary Thomas acknowledged how his marriage had revealed his real self:

I found there was a tremendous amount of immaturity within me that my marriage directly confronted. The key was that I had to change my view of marriage. If the purpose of marriage was simply to enjoy an infatuation and make me "happy," then I'd have to get a "new" marriage every two or three years. But if I really wanted to see God transform me from the inside out, I'd need to concentrate on changing myself rather than changing my spouse. In fact, you might even say, the more difficult my spouse proved to be, the more opportunity I'd have to grow.[1]

This shift in focus can transform your marriage. Rather than concentrating on your needs and your mate's faults, seeing the difficulties of your life together as an opportunity for *your* growth can be life-altering. Paying more attention to your own unloving ways can bring new life into your relationship. This is not easy to do. It is our natural bent to look out for ourselves and justify our own behavior.

My marriage has exposed my selfishness more than any other relationship of my life. The intimate day-to-day relating brings to light my own patterns that need changing if I am to grow as a human being. Earlier in our marriage, I had expectations I needed to surrender in order to rid myself of chronic disappointment and treat my husband more respectfully. In turn he needed to reevaluate his priority of work over family to reengage in a more balanced, loving way. The demands of marriage required both of us to change. Though painful at times, our awareness that we were in a process of becoming the people God designed us to be kept us moving forward.

In Ephesians 5:25–33 we are called to love each other in a way that will transform us. Husbands, who seem to struggle more with selfishness and lack of consideration, are exhorted to love their wives sacrificially. They are called to give themselves up for their wives just as Christ gave himself up for the church. Wives, who wrestle more with disappointment, are challenged to respect their husband. They are to esteem their husband and lift him up by affirming his adequacy. Husbands and wives are both asked to love in the way that is most difficult for them—sacrificing and respecting. That which is most difficult for us to do is what is required if we are to grow to love as Christ loves.

You are not on your own in this journey toward becoming a more loving, mature person. God has a vested interest in helping you grow. He loves you and wants to transform you from the inside out.[2] And he has the power to make that happen. Ephesians 3:20 tells us God is "able to do immeasurably more than all we ask or imagine, according to his power that is at work within us." He has the power to change you, your mate, and your marriage.

Do you want this kind of change for your marriage? Would you like to experience God's help in the transformation of your heart and behaviors in a way that will breathe new life into your marriage? If this is something you desire, it can happen through a relationship with God.

The Bible tells us that God is very relational and desires to have a personal relationship with you.[3] Through a relationship with him, you will experience love in its greatest form.[4] This love is amazingly freeing and powerful. Through it, you can see yourself in a new light. As you grow to see and love yourself differently, you will be able to offer glimmers of this love to your mate. (If this relationship is something you desire, see appendix D.)

When you married, you may have read from the "love chapter" of the Bible:

Love is patient, love is kind. It does not envy, it does not boast, it is not proud. It does not dishonor others, it is not self-seeking, it is not easily angered, it keeps no record of wrongs. Love does not delight in evil but rejoices with the truth. It always protects, always trusts, always hopes, always perseveres. Love never fails. (1 Cor. 13:4–8)

Loving like this is a tall order. I can look back on just the past week and realize I have not loved well. As a mere human, I am unable to love like this. I need God's love in me, changing my heart, to help me love well.

How does experiencing God's love change you and give you freedom to love your mate in new ways? Several come to mind.

Freedom to Admit

Knowing you are loved enables you to admit your own unloving behaviors. It creates a security that allows you to look at yourself honestly. The prideful and defensive parts of you that usually keep you from wanting to acknowledge fault can calm and over time be replaced with an increased capacity to see the "plank in your own eye."[5]

There is safety in discovering there is nothing you can do that would make God love you any less.[6] You don't need to hide who you truly are. God knows all about our self-centered ways and he loves us regardless. He wants us to acknowledge our unloving behavior and thoughts so that we can move past them.[7] He wants us to be free to live a life of love. Admitting our shortcomings allows us to release our old ways and experience his gracious love.

When your spouse is being snarky because they are having a bad day, rather than seeing their behavior or remarks as a personal slight, you have more space inside to see that this is about them, not you.

Freedom from Reactivity

Knowing you are loved by the One who made you gives you a firm place to stand regardless of how your mate is treating you. Your protectors can rest assured that you are safe inside God's love. When your spouse is being snarky because they are having a bad day, rather than seeing their behavior or remarks as a personal slight, you have more space inside to see that this is about them, not you. Their protectors are likely acting up, and you can choose to give your mate room to calm their internal struggle.

Freedom to Forgive

The verb *forgive* is defined in the dictionary as "to pardon an offense or an offender or to cancel or remit a debt."[8] From a Christian perspective, forgiveness is dramatically more exciting. A beautiful picture of forgiveness is found in the parable of the prodigal son, where the younger brother has wounded the heart of his father to the core by squandering his inheritance on raunchy living.[9]

When the young man returned home, he expected to be treated as less than a servant. Instead, his father ran out to meet him, embraced him, and lavished on him his love and a great feast. His forgiveness was far more than dutiful; it was extravagant. The story provides a picture of the abundant love God has for us, the generous nature of his forgiveness. It also invites us to become extravagant forgivers ourselves.

The concept of forgiveness can be hard to swallow. It makes sense that in the course of marriage we will need to forgive our mate over and over to move forward and enjoy a restored relationship after each fight or hurtful encounter. But being forgiven by God is a different story. You may feel you've led a pretty good life and, frankly, you don't feel the need to be forgiven. By the world's standard that may be true. But by God's standard, all of us have rejected him at some level. We all have dismissed God to some extent and tried to live life without him. We have relied on our protectors to get us through. This is what we all need forgiveness for—ignoring him.[10]

His forgiveness is freeing. When I want to make my husband pay for a mean comment he made or important moment he forgot, I remember that God has forgiven me for far more and my heart is softened. I will communicate my hurt but I no longer want to extract my pound of flesh. Forgiveness is like taking a weight off, allowing us to love with a lighter heart.

Freedom from Fear

As you experience the security of God's love for you, the fears that stir your protectors will lessen. Psalm 18:2 says, "My God is my rock, in whom I take refuge, my shield . . . my stronghold." As you grow in awareness of his strength, you will learn to trust that he is your greatest protector. You have less need to fear as you gain confidence in his presence and provision for you.

You also worry less about your needs getting met or not having what you need in the future, as you know your future is in his caring hands.[11] Knowing he's got your back, you can live in a less anxious, more openhearted way, enjoying the present.

Fear causes us to hide and guard ourselves. As we grow in our awareness that there is nothing that can separate us from God's love,[12] we are released to be vulnerable in our relationships with our spouse and others, knowing that we are ultimately safe in our relationship with him. When our mate hurts or disappoints us, we can extend trust more quickly, realizing that human love will always disappoint in some regard. We have more realistic expectations of our spouse's capacity to love us perfectly, and can lean into God's unfailing love.[13]

If we set out to change our mate we will likely become frustrated and disappointed. It is a strange and beautiful thing that it is when we feel fully accepted and loved that change becomes possible. When we feel accepted by God, we can open ourselves to exploring our self-protective ways of being with less threat. When we bring that same acceptance to our mate, assuring them that despite their stumbling our love for them is secure, they are free to look at themselves with less defensiveness and change can begin. It is no wonder that this most exposing relationship also carries with it the seeds of the most transformational opportunity of our lives.

Discussion Questions: Chapter 11

Group and Couple Questions

1. Has your marriage been a catalyst for growth for you personally? If so, how? Read 2 Corinthians 3:16–18, Ephesians 3:20, and Proverbs 27:17. What do these verses say about how God is at work in your life and, consequently, your marriage?

2. Read Ephesians 5:25-33. What makes it difficult for a husband to sacrifice himself for the sake of his wife? What makes it difficult for a wife to respect her husband? Do you think husbands struggle more with selfishness and wives struggle more with disappointment? How must each surrender something in order to love well? What is one thing you can do this week to love your wife sacrificially or demonstrate respect for your husband?

3. Read 1 John 4:9–16. How is God's love shown to us? Formed in us? Have you experienced the freedom his love makes possible in your relationship? (The freedom to admit? The freedom from reactivity? The freedom to forgive? The freedom from fear?) Can you think of other ways that his love has freed or can free you to love differently?

For Personal Reflection

1. When you got married, did you expect that you would have to change? Did you consider yourself to be selfish when you got married? Would you say that marriage has given you an opportunity to look more realistically at your tendency to be selfish?

2. Read 1 John 4:9–16. How does God's love for you release you to love your mate more fully? How does his love for you give you the security you need to live more freely? Have you experienced more freedom in any of the four ways mentioned in the chapter?

12

Better Together

Chains do not hold a marriage together. It is threads, hundreds of tiny threads which sew people together through the years.

Simone Signoret

You and your mate have a shared story. How you met, what first attracted you to each other, the adjustments of married life, the birth of children, adventures you've enjoyed, hardships you've weathered together—all combine to make up your mutual history, threads that hold you together through the years.

What are your threads? Think back to your early days of courtship. What drew you to one another? What did you see in your mate that began to connect your heart to theirs? What did you do that began to bring you together? Was it going out to dinner, hiking, listening to music, playing a sport, taking a class? What shared memories did you create? What made you laugh? What were your inside jokes? What was your first trip together? What were your terms of affection?

Many simple things form the strength of the bond you share—laughing, crying, long conversations, enjoying a sunset. Each of these is a thread that connects you together through the years. There are also major threads such as the birth of your children, buying a home, or the joys and heartaches you've experienced as a couple. Even your most serious conflicts and negative experiences can serve as threads as you endure and overcome.

Your shared history is a sustaining force for lasting love. These experiences are a treasure that can serve as collateral as you face difficult times in your married life.

If you have been married less than ten years, it is likely you are still building that collateral. You have put in a great deal of effort but may not yet be reaping the full reward. Mark Twain once observed, "Love seems the swiftest, but it is the slowest of all growths. No man or woman really knows what perfect love is until they have been married a quarter of a century."[1] It takes time to build that shared history and enjoy the benefits of your investment. Unfortunately, some young couples choose to bail out of their marriages before they have had a chance to enjoy the fruit of their perseverance.

Looking Forward

When you began reading this book, you may have felt hopeless or at least seriously discouraged about your marriage, with no belief that things could possibly change between you and your spouse. You are not alone. Most marriages experience times, or even prolonged seasons, that are painful and seem impassable.

It is helpful at these times to both rehearse your shared history and think ahead to what you hope for in your relationship. It may be hard to picture today what the two of you can make of your marriage, but I would encourage you to begin to cast a vision for what can be.

You both have longings and desires for life ahead. You have personal goals as well as marital and family goals. You have ideas about how you would like to treat each other, what you want to do for recreation, and how you'd like to shape the character and competencies of your children.

It can help to create a new, shared vision with your mate, a "marriage vision"[2] that will help you define your intentions for the future and inspire you toward experiencing a thriving relationship. To do this, set aside unpressured time when the two of you can do some brainstorming. Choose a time when you are fresh and free of cell phones, kids, and so forth.

Begin by each making a list of goals you want to see happen in your marriage. State each one positively, as if it were already happening. Here is a sample list:

We are affectionate.

We respect each other.

We have a weekly date night.

We take time to notice our protectors during or after a conflict.

We are compassionate toward young parts in ourselves and each other.

We enjoy sex.

We laugh together.

We express appreciation at least once per day.

We have daily couple time.

When one of us is away, we stay in daily contact.

We make collaborative decisions.

We prioritize each other over parents, extended family, and friends.

We nurture our spiritual lives.

Once you make your list, share it with your mate. Put a plus symbol next to any goals you both agree are important. Make a new, combined list including all goals you both think are important.

Then review the list and be more specific. Identify two to three strategies or behaviors that will accomplish each item. For instance:

1. We make collaborative decisions.
   a. When determining where we will spend the holidays, we talk together and agree on our schedule. We do not commit to our families in any way until we have fully agreed as a couple.
   b. When making a purchase over $200, we consult each other first.

2. We have daily couple time.
   a. After the kids are down, we take thirty minutes to unwind together and share about our day or concerns.
   b. During couple time, we shut off our phones, television, and so forth, and give each other our undivided attention.

This combined list of goals and strategies becomes your marriage vision. Post the goals of your vision someplace where you will see them daily. Review your complete list of strategies weekly until it becomes part of your DNA as a couple. Remember, this is a living document you can change or add to as time goes on.

Creating a shared marriage vision will help you know where you're headed and help you stay on course when life starts to pull you off course. The vision will empower you to change by keeping you mindful of your goals as a couple. If there are one or more items that one of you felt were very important but the other didn't, make a note of those items and, at another time, use the skills provided in chapter 6 to address them together.

Becoming Your Best Together

We are all in the process of becoming. The spouse you see today is not the spouse you will see in the future. My husband and I have been married for forty years. We had no idea how much we would both change through the ups and downs of life together. The selfishness that characterized our early years of marriage has given way to a willingness to give and compromise. The tendency to seek to satisfy our own needs first has given way to a mutually supportive concern with meeting the needs of both of us. We still have our selfish moments, but we each recognize them and are able to apologize and change course more quickly.

Are you feeling discouraged about your marriage and the prospects for change? God's got this. He is in the business of transformation. He wants you to experience the joys of marriage even more than you do. After all, it was his idea.

As I look back on the seasons of our married life, there were times when the only thing holding our marriage together was the commitment we'd made to stick it out. One such season was when my husband was questioning his love for me. I was devastated and hurt. Knowing I was loved by God was an anchor for me during that time. I was able to find peace in the midst of my husband's confusion and not react out of fear or hurt.

Although I was tempted to push him away and protect myself from further pain, I was able to stay centered in my relationship with God as my husband sorted through his emotions. Then, when he did express his desire to restore our relationship, I was tempted to punish him. But after I reflected on how much my loving God had forgiven me, it was hard to justify holding out on forgiveness for my husband.

We are all in the process of becoming who we were made to be. If you can see your mate as someone in process instead of a static set of negative traits, you will open up a space for them to grow.

God's love softens hearts and makes restoration possible. Having an intimate relationship with God changes the way you see yourself (as fully known and fully loved) and your mate (as a work in progress in the hands of a loving God). When loving God is your priority, knowing how to love the other becomes clear. It becomes easier to allow the space and time for God to work in their life and in yours.

We are all in the process of becoming who we were made to be. If you can see your mate as someone in process instead of a static set of negative traits, you will open up a space for them to grow. When you yourself have been given this space by God, who sees your "warts" and loves you still, you are more able to offer the space to others. You can help your spouse become all God desires them to be.

Tim Keller says:

> Within this Christian vision of marriage, here's what it means to fall in love. It is to look at another person and get a glimpse of what God is creating, and to say, "I see who God is making you, and it excites me! I want to be part of that. I want to partner with you and God in the journey you are taking to his throne. And when we get there, I will look at your magnificence and say, 'I always knew you could be like this. I got glimpses of it on earth, but now look at you!'"[3]

What a tremendous opportunity we have to witness our mate becoming all they were meant to be. Your marriage is a work in progress. Together, you and your mate share a venture that is unique in all the world. No two people are like you. No two have more potential to shape each other into their best selves than do you.

■ ■ ■

When you said "I do," you likely had no idea that the journey that lay ahead would involve as many roadblocks and potholes as you have discovered. Your picture then did not include the detours and road construction that would be necessary. You couldn't have anticipated the personal makeovers that would need to occur as self-centered ways of thinking and being are exposed and molted to allow love to grow.

Marriage was designed by God to meet our deepest needs for companionship and intimacy. It was also designed to be our place of most profound transformation. We cannot enjoy the heights of the first without experiencing the metamorphosis of the latter. I hope you embrace the adventure. There are vistas ahead you cannot imagine.

Discussion Questions: Chapter 12

Group and Couple Questions

1. Share with your group the highlights of your shared history. You might include how you met, how you became engaged, funny moments, difficult seasons, and so forth. What are your significant "threads"?

2. Create your "Marriage Vision" by following the directions in the chapter. Share with the group two of your goals and two or three strategies that you intend to implement to meet those goals. If you are comfortable, invite them to hold you accountable to working toward those goals by checking in on your progress occasionally.

3. Read the quote by Tim Keller aloud. Share with your mate the "glimpses of magnificence" you have been able to see in them, evidences of God's work in their life. Discuss together how you can hinder God's activity in each other (stir up protectors) and how you can support his work in each other's lives.

4. Read 2 Thessalonians 3:5. If your heart was filled with God's love and Christ's perseverance, how would that impact your marriage? Your tenacity during hard times? What is the relationship between love and perseverance?

For Personal Reflection

1. How does it help to think of your mate as being "a work in progress" rather than defining them by their negative traits? How might such a gracious attitude align with how God sees you? Read Romans 5:8. Does God wait till we are perfect to love us? What implications does your answer have for loving your mate?

2. What are the "glimpses of magnificence" you can see in your partner today? If you can't see them, look harder. God sees them and he wants you to share his vision. If you do see them, savor them and know there are more to come!

Appendix A

Feeling Words

Anxious: stressed, jittery, on edge, apprehensive, antsy, distressed, fidgety, hyper, jumpy, nervous, restless, shaky, unglued, uptight, wired, uneasy, agitated, tense

Peaceful: calm, serene, settled, restful, quiet, collected, composed, mellow, still, unruffled, untroubled, tranquil, pensive

Fearful: filled with dread, afraid, disturbed, frightened, fainthearted, hesitant, panicky, scared, uneasy, worried

Joyful: exuberant, happy, excited, cheerful, delighted, ecstatic, elated, glad, festive, enraptured, gratified, lighthearted, overjoyed, jubilant, pleased, pleasurable, upbeat

Resentful: bitter, displeased, injured, dismayed, antagonistic, hurt, indignant, maligned, offended, perturbed, spiteful, vexed, pessimistic

Grateful: thankful, gracious, appreciative, openhearted, content, full, gratified

Frustrated: irritated, annoyed, bothered, exasperated, defeated, discouraged, disheartened, irked, stonewalled, stymied, stifled, discontent

Playful: frisky, carefree, fun-loving, light, cheerful, childlike, mischievous, lively, spirited, whimsical

Angry: furious, rageful, wrathful, peeved, antagonistic, cross, displeased, enraged, fierce, fiery, fuming, hateful, heated, hot, incensed, infuriated, irate, outraged, provoked, riled

Connected: close, intimate, belonging, valued, desirable, joined, together, united

Lonely: alone, misunderstood, abandoned, deserted, rejected, apart, undesirable, unloved, uninteresting, estranged, forsaken, isolated, friendless, withdrawn, disconnected

Loving: compassionate, tender, caring, affectionate, attached, devoted, fond, loyal, respectful, romantic, warmhearted

Guilty: at fault, responsible, convicted, bad, accused, condemned, wrong, judged, burdened

Apologetic: sorry, remorseful, contrite, regretful

Sad: depressed, down, blue, grieved, despondent, bereaved, dejected, despairing, distressed, dismal, gloomy, heartbroken, heavyhearted, low, melancholy, morose, sorrowful

Invalidated: discounted, dismissed, unimportant, overlooked, devalued, discredited, negated, overruled, undermined

Shameful: dirty, unlovable, bad, damaged, defective, unwanted, stained, judged, unworthy, flawed, rejected, wrong, self-hating, exposed, tainted, pathetic, disgraceful, humiliated

Appendix B

Sample List of Protectors

I. *Preemptive Protectors* (also known as *Managers*). They try to anticipate and act in advance of any problem surfacing. Their motto is "Never again." Never again do they want you to feel the painful feelings or longings of childhood. They intercept them through various tactics.

   a. Avoider—don't engage so you won't have to feel.

   b. Analyst—keep a safe distance by observing and critiquing.

   c. Skeptic—distrust to stay safe.

   d. Striver—push yourself to prove you're worthy.

   e. Pleaser—make others happy so you are loved.

   f. Soldier—just get through it and do your duty.

   g. Distance/Closeness Regulator—pull others toward you or push them away to feel okay.

   h. Explainer—justify your position to ensure you're okay.

   i. Superior One—claim to be a cut above to ensure you are invulnerable.

   j. Judge—condemn to keep others or yourself in check.

   k. Shamer—humiliate in order to keep hidden.

l. Passive One—keep safe by showing yourself to no one.

m. Victim—avoid responsibility by blaming others.

n. Anxious One—stay vigilant to ensure safety.

o. Distractor—divert attention to ensure safety.

p. Contemptuous One—display disdain to avoid vulnerability.

q. Planner—focus on future plans to avoid present pain.

r. Controller—constrict environment or others to manage feelings.

s. Caretaker—care for others to avoid own feelings.

II. *Reactive Protectors* (also known as *Firefighters*). They sound the alarm when Managers have failed to keep the painful feelings in check. They seize control and make sure the feelings and longings of childhood, as expressed by the young parts, are extinguished.

a. Angry One—vent or protest to protect your vulnerability.

b. Substance User—numb to avoid pain.

c. Addicted One—numb to avoid pain.

d. Disconnector—dissociate, numb, get foggy, or get sleepy to cut off from pain.

e. Suicidal One—harm self to avoid pain.

f. Self-Mutilator—harm self to avoid or soothe pain.

g. Sexual Binger—use sex to avoid pain.

h. Binge Eater—binge eat to distract from pain.

i. Food Restricter—restrict food intake to distract from pain.

j. High Risk–Taker—do extreme things to deaden pain.

k. Obsessive One—extreme focus to avoid painful feelings.

l. Violent One—lash out to avoid feelings.

I am indebted to Richard Schwartz, author of *Internal Family Systems Therapy* (New York: Guilford Press, 1995), for his origination of the concept of protector parts.

Appendix C

Renewal of Covenant Marriage

If you would like to renew your marriage vows with a new understanding of covenant, here's one way you might consider doing so.

Renewing your vows can be an intimate expression between just the two of you and God, a commitment you make in the presence of your children, or an event you invite others to witness. Choose a location such as your bedroom, your backyard, a favorite outdoor spot, or a chapel. If you are renewing your vows privately, make sure the time is protected from interruption—no kids, phones, and so forth.

1. Plan ahead how you would like to share your renewed vows.

   a. If you have a copy of your original vows, and they include the idea of covenant, you might simply want to restate your vows with a new awareness of the meaning of covenant.

   b. You may want to rewrite your vows, including the idea of covenant. The marriage covenant is an enduring, total commitment that says, "This is how I will always be toward you." No matter what happens, it is a promise to love regardless. Traditional vows include this idea of permanency: "I take you to be my lawful and wedded [husband], and I do promise and covenant, before God and these witnesses, to be your loving and faithful [wife]. In plenty and in want, in joy and in sorrow, in sickness and in health, as long as we both shall live."

2. Speak your vows to one another. Hold hands, look into each other's eyes, and say your vows.

3. Optional: to symbolically represent your new commitment, you may want to set up three candles. After your vows you can light the two side candles, which represent the two of you—your unique selves with all your gifting, personalities, wounds, abilities—in short, your total selves. As you light your candle, take a moment to reflect on the flame as it represents all that is you.

   After a few moments, take your individual candles and together light the center candle. Lighting the center candle is saying "I do" to the covenant promise to love your spouse for your lifetime. It represents your union with one another, two becoming one. This idea is derived from Jesus's words, "For this reason a man will leave his father and mother and be united to his wife, and the two will become one flesh. So they are no longer two, but one" (Matt. 19:5–6).

   You may choose to blow out each of the individual candles, knowing both your flames burn now in the center candle. Or you may choose to blow out your candle and then relight your mate's candle as they relight yours, to represent your mutual commitment to bring the best out in the other, to help them become all God intends them to be.

4. Celebrate!

Appendix D

Beginning a Personal Relationship with God

What if there was a perfect lover out there? What if there was one who knew you intimately and loved you passionately for exactly who you are? What if this one would never fail you, never leave you, always have your best interest at heart? Would you want that kind of lover?

The Bible tells us that's exactly who God is. It says he made you,[1] knows you completely,[2] and loves you more than you can imagine.[3] It also says that God is a completely trustworthy lover.[4] He will never pull back or withdraw his love, no matter what. You can be real with him, because there is nothing you can do that will separate you from his love.[5] He knows you and you can know him. No hiding, no pretending, no worrying about being something you're not. There's nothing you can do to make him love you more, and nothing you can do to make him love you less. It is settled.

The Bible says God wants to be known by you as you are known by him.[6] To reveal himself to you and to demonstrate his love for you, he sent his own Son into the world in the person of Jesus.[7]

The Bible also says that we, as humans, all suffer from the same problem. We have a built-in tendency to try to make our own lives work without God. The Bible calls this *sin*, which is the same as saying "independence from God." This independence separates us from God—it creates a gap between us and God. Jesus came to bridge that gap and he did so by taking on himself the penalty of our willful independence by dying on the cross.[8] In doing so he opened the way for us to enjoy a restored relationship with God, now and forever.

Our protectors urge us to remain independent of God. They have wooed us with false promises of finding life apart from him. They cannot satisfy what our hearts yearn for. Our selves are hungry for God. As God invites us into relationship with himself, we can ask for forgiveness for allowing our protectors to lead us and for having relinquished control to them.

Entering a relationship with God involves believing in Jesus[9] (believe that God sent him, that he died for you, and that God raised him from death), asking for his forgiveness[10] (acknowledging that your own efforts to make your life work without God haven't worked), and receiving him into your heart.[11] In so doing, in a mysterious way, Jesus now lives in you.[12] To do this, you can simply talk to God in prayer.

When you believe and receive Jesus, you will find yourself to be more open to the love God has for you. You can now live out of your "new creation,"[13] the self that is now in Christ. As you grow closer to him through time spent with him in prayer and reading his Word (the Bible), you will find yourself drawn to love him, yourself, your mate, and others more.[14] You will have found your true Soul Mate.

Appendix E

Infographic of Survey Results

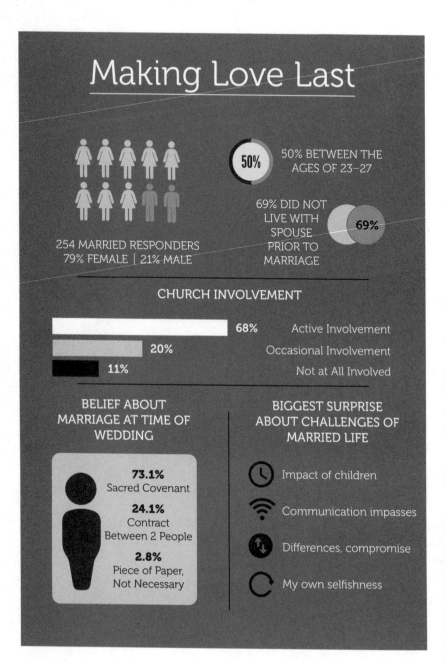

Making Love Last

254 MARRIED RESPONDERS
79% FEMALE | 21% MALE

50% 50% BETWEEN THE AGES OF 23–27

69% DID NOT LIVE WITH SPOUSE PRIOR TO MARRIAGE **69%**

CHURCH INVOLVEMENT

68% Active Involvement

20% Occasional Involvement

11% Not at All Involved

BELIEF ABOUT MARRIAGE AT TIME OF WEDDING

73.1%
Sacred Covenant

24.1%
Contract
Between 2 People

2.8%
Piece of Paper,
Not Necessary

BIGGEST SURPRISE ABOUT CHALLENGES OF MARRIED LIFE

Impact of children

Communication impasses

Differences, compromise

My own selfishness

Notes

Chapter 1 Why Marriage Is Hard Work

1. U.S. Department of Health and Human Services, "First Marriages in the United States: Data from the 2006–2010 National Survey of Family Growth," *National Health Statistics Reports* no. 49 (March 22, 2012), http://www.cdc.gov/nchs/data/nhsr/nhsr049.pdf.

2. David Popenoe and Barbara Dafoe Whitehead, "Why Men Won't Commit: Exploring Young Men's Attitudes about Sex, Dating and Marriage," *The State of Our Unions 2002: The Social Health of Marriage in America*, ed. by David Popenoe and Barbara Dafoe Whitehead (Piscataway, NJ: Rutgers University National Marriage Project, 2002), 12, http://www.stateofourunions.org/pdfs/SOOU2002.pdf.

3. "Wedding Money: What Does the Average Wedding Cost?" *The Knot*, accessed November 17, 2016, https://www.theknot.com/content/what-does-the-average-wedding-cost.

Chapter 2 More Than You Imagined

1. Laura Taggart, "Making Love Last," survey conducted through Survey Monkey, September to December 2015. Survey distributed through social media to individuals married ten years or less.

2. This concept of marriage as merger or start-up is also found in Charles Murray, *The Curmudgeon's Guide to Getting Ahead* (New York: Crown Business, 2014), 137–40.

3. Dan Gilbert, "The Surprising Science of Happiness," *TED Talks*, February 2004, https://www.ted.com/talks/dan_gilbert_asks_why_are_we_happy?

4. Tim Keller, *The Meaning of Marriage* (New York: Dutton, 2011), 35.

5. Yasmin Anway, "Science of Happiness MOOC Captivates Millennials," *Berkeley News*, June 30, 2014, http://news.berkeley.edu/2014/06/30/science-of-happiness-mooc/.

6. Philippians 1:6; 2:13.

7. Song of Songs chapters 4–5; Proverbs 5:18–19; Ephesians 5:25–33.

Notes

Chapter 3 Why Marriage Is Worth It

1. Linda J. Waite et al., *Does Divorce Make People Happy? Findings from a Study of Unhappy Marriages* (New York: Institute for American Values, 2002), http://americanvalues.org/catalog/pdfs/does_divorce_make_people_happy.pdf.
2. John Gottman, *The Seven Principles for Making Marriage Work* (New York: Three Rivers Press, 1999), 5.
3. Dr. Norval Glenn, "With This Ring: A National Survey on Marriage in America," (National Fatherhood Initiative, 2005), http://wyofams.org/index_htm_files/NationalMarriageSurvey.pdf.
4. National Institute of Mental Health, "Anxiety Disorders," *NIMH* (May 2015), http://www.nimh.nih.gov/health/topics/anxiety-disorders/index.shtml.
5. Henri J. M. Nouwen, *Reaching Out: The Three Movements of the Spiritual Life* (New York: Doubleday, 1975), 71–72.
6. Romans 5:8.
7. 1 Chronicles 16:34; John 3:16; 1 John 3:1.
8. Psalm 13:5; Hebrews 13:5.
9. I am indebted to Ellyn Bader and Peter Pearson of the Couples Institute for their developmental approach to treating couples in therapy. I have adapted their ideas from "Stepping Stones to Intimacy: A Positive Outlook on Problems," accessed May 7, 2016, http://www.couplesinstitute.com/stepping-stones-to-intimacy-a-positive-outlook-on-problems-in-couples-relationships/.
10. Ibid.
11. 2 Corinthians 3:18; 5:17; Romans 12:2.
12. Bader and Pearson, "Stepping Stones to Intimacy."
13. This concept of the stock market as an analogy for marriage is also found in Fred Lowery, *Covenant Marriage: Staying Together for Life* (West Monroe, LA: Howard, 2002), 222–23.

Chapter 4 Search Yourself

1. Ephesians 2:4–8.
2. I am indebted to Richard Schwartz, author of *Internal Family Systems Therapy* (New York: Guilford Press, 1995), for his conceptualization of internal parts.
3. Frederick Buechner, *Telling Secrets* (New York: HarperCollins, 1991), 45.
4. And that self is never more authentic than when we live in a consciously dependent relationship with God. Without that relationship we easily get pushed and pulled by the agendas of others and our own self-protective parts, our other selves. Self is ungrounded and incomplete when not tethered to its divine source.
5. Schwartz, *Internal Family Systems Therapy*, 96.
6. This "tracking sequence" is adapted from Toni Herbine-Blank, *Intimacy from the Inside Out* (New York: Routledge, 2016), 39–49.
7. Schwartz, *Internal Family Systems Therapy*, 108–10.
8. Matthew 19:13–14.
9. Psalm 46:1.
10. Isaiah 61:1.
11. 1 John 3:1; Psalm 139; Isaiah 66:13.
12. Schwartz, *Internal Family Systems Therapy*, 49–51.

258

13. This template is adapted from Herbine-Blank, "Tracking Sequences Meditation," *Intimacy from the Inside Out.*

14. Jay Earley, *Self Therapy* (Larksburg, CA: Pattern System Books, 2009), 114–16.

15. Henri Nouwen notes, "Too often we will do everything possible to avoid the confrontation with the experience of being alone, and sometimes we are able to create the most ingenious devices to prevent ourselves from being reminded of this condition . . . we panic when there is nothing or nobody left to distract us. When we have no project to finish, no friend to visit . . . no television to watch . . . and when we are left all alone by ourselves we are brought so close to the revelation of our basic human aloneness and are so afraid of experiencing an all-pervasive sense of loneliness that we will do anything to get busy again and continue the game which makes us believe that everything is fine after all" (Nouwen, *Reaching Out,* 26–27).

16. Colossians 1:22.

17. This is, in a nutshell, what the Bible calls *sin*—trying to make our life work without God.

18. The original source of this quote is unknown, but it is widely attributed to Carl Jung and may be from one of his many speaking engagements.

Chapter 5 Embrace Differences

1. Louann Brizendine, *The Female Brain* (New York: Harmony Books, 2006), 5.

2. M. Ingalhalikar et al., "Sex Differences in the Structural Connectome of the Human Brain," *Proceedings of the National Academy of Sciences* 111(2) (December 2013): 823–28; Ariel Niu, "Gender & the Brain: Differences between Women & Men," *Fit Brains,* February 18, 2014, http://www.fitbrains.com/blog/women-men-brains/.

3. Ibid.

4. Brizendine, *The Female Brain,* 5.

5. Ibid., 91.

6. John Gray, *Men Are from Mars, Women Are from Venus* (New York: Harper-Collins, 1992), 132–49.

7. Loyola University Health System, "What Falling in Love Does to Your Heart and Brain," *Science Daily,* February 6, 2014, https://www.sciencedaily.com/releases/2014/02/140206155244.htm.

8. Dietrich Bonhoeffer, *Life Together* (New York: Harper and Row, 1954), 101.

Chapter 6 Tackle Conflict

1. Taggart, "Making Love Last" survey.

2. Gottman, *Seven Principles for Making Marriage Work,* 130.

3. Daniel B. Wile, *After the Honeymoon* (Oakland, CA: Daniel Wile, 2008), 13.

4. Herbine-Blank, *Intimacy from the Inside Out,* 57.

5. Originally developed by Thomas Gordon, *Parent Effectiveness Training* (New York: Three Rivers, 2000).

6. Gottman, *Seven Principles for Making Marriage Work,* 38.

7. Ibid., 130–32.

8. J. Carlson, D. Dinkmeyer, and D. Dinkmeyer Sr., *Time for a Better Marriage* (Atascadero, CA: Impact Publishers, 2003), 87.

9. Keller, *Meaning of Marriage*, 138.

Chapter 7 Let Go

1. Hilary White, "24 Signs You've Found Your Soul Mate," *PopSugar*, November 3, 2016, http://www.popsugar.com/love/Signs-Youve-Found-Your-Soul-Mate-35421825.

2. Offering an invitation at the conclusion of the tracking sequence is the contribution of Toni Herbine-Blank, *Intimacy from the Inside Out,* 46–47.

3. Brene Brown, *I Thought It Was Just Me, But It Isn't* (New York: Avery/Penguin, 2007), 5.

4. Helen Keller, *Let Us Have Faith* (New York: Doubleday Doran, 1940).

Chapter 8 Lean In

1. Gottman, *Seven Principles for Making Marriage Work*, 80.

2. William Larkin, MD, "Build Your 'Gratitude Brain,'" *The Applied Neuroscience Blog*, October 5, 2015, http://appliedneuroscienceblog.com/build-your-gratitude-brain.

3. John Powell, *The Secret of Staying in Love* (Thomas More, 1995), 55.

4. S. H. Kim, Y. H. Kim, and H. J. Kim, "Laughter and Stress Relief in Cancer Patients: A Pilot Study," *Evidence-Based Complementary and Alternative Medicine* (2015), http://www.hindawi.com/journals/ecam/2015/864739/.

5. George Bonanno, "Loss, Trauma, and Human Resilience," *American Psychologist* (January 2004): 20–28.

6. Virginia Satir, "Virginia Satir Quotes," BrainyQuote.com, accessed December 1, 2016, https://www.brainyquote.com/quotes/quotes/v/virginiasa175185.html.

7. Karen Grewen and Kathleen Light, "More Frequent Partner Hugs and Higher Oxytocin Levels Are Linked to Lower Blood Pressure and Heart Rate in Premenopausal Women," *Biological Psychology* 69 (April 2005): 5–21.

8. Dacher Keltner, "Hands on Research: The Science of Touch," *Greater Good: The Science of a Meaningful Life* (September 29, 2010), http://greatergood.berkeley.edu/article/item/hands_on_research.

9. Adapted from Ken Sande, *The Peacemaker: A Biblical Guide to Resolving Personal Conflict*, third ed. (Grand Rapids: Baker Books, 2004), 126–33.

10. "The heart's fierce effort to protect itself from every slight, to shield its touchy honor from the bad opinion of friend and enemy, will never let the mind have rest." For a brilliant explanation of pride versus meekness, see A. W. Tozer, *The Pursuit of God* (Camp Hill, PA: Christian Publications, 1982), 105–7.

11. Matthew 7:3–5.

12. Keller, *Meaning of Marriage*, 165.

Chapter 9 Initiate Intimacy

1. Psalm 139:1–4; John 17:23, 26.

2. Genesis 2:22–24.

3. Genesis 2:25.

4. Michele Weiner Davis, *The Sex-Starved Marriage* (New York: Simon and Schuster, 2003), 33.

5. Brizendine, *The Female Brain*, 68.

6. Dario Nardi, "Hormones, Sex and Personality Type," *Bulletin of Psychological Type* 26, no. 3 (2003): 22–24.

7. Marie S. Carmichael et al., "Plasma Oxytocin Increases in the Human Sexual Response," *The Journal of Clinical Endocrinology and Metabolism* 64, no. 1 (January 1987): 27–31.

8. Brizendine, *The Female Brain*, 71.

9. 1 Corinthians 7:3–5.

10. Clifford and Joyce Penner, *Restoring the Pleasure* (Nashville: Thomas Nelson, 2016), 46.

11. Norman Doidge, *The Brain That Changes Itself* (New York: Viking, 2007), 20.

12. D. H. Angres and K. Bettinardi-Angres, "The Disease of Addiction: Origins, Treatment, and Recovery," *Disease-a-Month* 54 (2008): 696–721.

13. James G. Pfaus et al., "Who, What, Where, When (and Maybe Even Why)? How the Experience of Sexual Reward Connects Sexual Desire, Preference, and Performance," *Archives of Sexual Behavior* 41 (2012): 31–62.

14. Omar Minwalla, "Thirteen Dimensions of Sex Addiction Induced Trauma among Partners and Spouses Impacted by Sex Addiction," *The Institute for Sexual Health*, April 2014.

15. Mark Laaser, *Healing the Wounds of Sexual Addiction* (Grand Rapids: Zondervan, 2004).

16. Dan Allender, *The Wounded Heart: Hope for Adult Victims of Childhood Sexual Abuse* (Colorado Springs: Navpress, 1995), 71.

17. Psalm 139:14; Isaiah 61:3.

18. Song of Songs 4:16–6:3.

19. Michael Castleman, "The Most Important Sexual Statistic," *Psychology Today*, March 16, 2009, https://www.psychologytoday.com/blog/all-about-sex /200903/the-most-important-sexual-statistic.

20. Laurie B. Mintz, "Female Orgasm: Time to Stop Shoulding Ourselves," *Psychology Today* (September 2012), https://www.psychologytoday.com/blog/stress -and-sex/201209/female-orgasm-time-stop-shoulding-ourselves.

21. Sheila Wray Gregoire, *The Good Girl's Guide to Great Sex* (Grand Rapids: Zondervan, 2012), 45.

22. Sam Storms, *More Precious Than Gold* (Wheaton: Crossway, 2009), 182.

23. Clifford and Joyce Penner, *The Way to Love Your Wife* (Colorado Springs: Focus on the Family, 2007), 5.

24. Brizendine, *The Female Brain*, 78.

25. Ibid., 77.

26. Gary Thomas, *Devotions for a Sacred Marriage* (Grand Rapids: Zondervan, 2005); Gary Chapman, *The One Year Love Language Minute Devotional* (Carol Stream, IL: Tyndale, 2009).

27. Keller, *Meaning of Marriage*.

Chapter 10 The Power of a Promise

1. Thornton Wilder, *Three Plays by Thornton Wilder: Our Town, The Skin of Our Teeth, The Matchmaker* (New York: Bantam Books, 1958), 113.

2. Genesis 17:7.

3. Daniel Brown, *Unlock the Power of Family: Discover God's Design for Lasting Relationships* (Sparrow Press, 1994), 54.

4. Ibid., 103.

5. Lew Smedes, "Controlling the Unpredictable—The Power of Promising," *Christianity Today*, January 1983, 3–4.

6. Ibid.

Chapter 11   Marriage as a Catalyst for Change

1. Gary Thomas, *Sacred Marriage* (Grand Rapids: Zondervan, 2000), 23.
2. 2 Corinthians 3:16–18.
3. 1 John 4:9–16.
4. 1 John 3:1; Ephesians 3:18.
5. Matthew 7:3–5.
6. Romans 8:38–39; Hebrews 13:5.
7. 1 John 1:9.
8. W. Nichols, S. Steinmetz, J. Sora, P. Edmunds, C. Levine, *Random House Webster's College Dictionary* (New York: Random House, 2000).
9. Luke 15:11–32.
10. Isaiah 53:6.
11. Jeremiah 29:11; Proverbs 3:5–6.
12. Romans 8:35–39.
13. Psalm 13:5.

Chapter 12   Better Together

1. Mark Twain, *Mark Twain's Notebook #22: The Complete Works of Mark Twain* (New York: Harper and Brothers, 1935).
2. Adapted from Harville Hendrix, *Getting the Love You Want* (New York: Harper and Row, 1988), 247–48.
3. Keller, *Meaning of Marriage*, 121.

Appendix D

1. Ephesians 2:10; Mark 10:6.
2. 1 Corinthians 13:12.
3. John 15:13; Galatians 2:20.
4. Hebrews 13:5.
5. Romans 8:38–39.
6. John 10:14.
7. Romans 5:8; 1 John 4:9–10.
8. Isaiah 53:6–8.
9. John 11:25.
10. 1 John 1:9.
11. John 1:12.
12. Colossians 1:27; John 17:20–26; 1 John 4:13–15.
13. 2 Corinthians 5:17.
14. 1 John 4:11-12.

Laura Taggart, MA, LMFT, is a marital therapist and supervisor at Community Presbyterian Counseling Center in San Ramon, California. She has served as director of counseling and director of marriage and family ministry for Community Presbyterian Church in Danville, California. She holds a master's degree from Fuller Theological Seminary, where she has served on the adjunct faculty. She is an adjunct professor for the Evangelical Theological College in Addis Ababa, Ethiopia. She lives in the San Francisco Bay Area with her husband.

LAURA TAGGART is a licensed marriage and family therapist who is passionate about helping couples get unstuck from negative patterns and learn to love each other well.

Connect with her online to

gain valuable insights from Laura's blog posts

sign up to receive updates via email

find out about Laura's speaking events

invite her to speak to your
church or other group

WWW.LAURATAGGART.COM

f LauraTaggart.LMFT

Are you *losing the love* you once felt for each other?

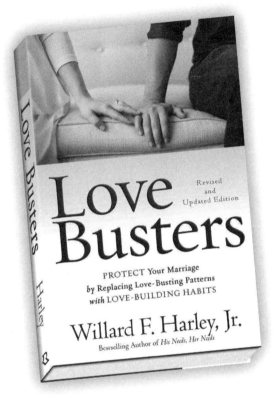

From Dr. Harley, the author of *His Needs, Her Needs*, comes a book that will help you identify the six Love Busters that pull marriages apart and will show you and your spouse how to avoid them. The strength of your marriage depends on the passion you share for each other. So stop destroying the feeling of love and discover, instead, how to build your love with care and with time.